Dt ᴧdvice

by

Chris Jary

First published by C P J Publishing 2011

A catalogue record for this book is available from the British
Library.

ISBN 978-0-9568431-0-4

Prepared and printed by:

York Publishing Services Ltd
64 Hallfield Road
Layerthorpe
York
YO31 7ZQ

Tel: 01904 431213

Website: www.yps-publishing.co.uk

This book is dedicated to two groups of people:

First of all my family who have helped me through times of illness, as well as financial hardship, but most of all for being there to listen when times have been tough, lonely and sometimes unbearable.

Mum your one in a million with the way you listen, always giving encouragement and you never seem to give any negative thoughts on my views and give me so much love; Dad, we've had our ups and downs, but thanks for listening as well as your support; Alison, nobody could ask for more from a sister and being there when needed; Kate and Sarah my daughters who I'm very proud of and live their lives to the full, Christine you're always there for our children as well as me, and finally Clare for your support and encouragement.

Secondly for my many friends and business acquaintances who, if it wasn't for their trust and belief in what I have achieved in the past as well as what I hope to accomplish in the future, I wouldn't be publishing this book today, so special thanks must go to:

- Owen Richardson of McLaren Financial

- Martin Cooper of Total Results Ltd

- Brian Wardell

- Amanda Dixon for her marketing ideas and suggestions

- John Walton for finalising the book

- Rudi for his contributions for the cartoons at very short notice

- Wendy –Many thanks

- Gerard Wood

And many more individuals within the networking groups throughout the North East especially Network North, IPN Connect etc. You have all helped and encouraged in your special ways.

This book is dedicated to two groups of people:

First of all my family who have helped me through times of illness, as well as financial hardship, but most of all for being there to listen when times have been tough, lonely and sometimes unbearable.

Mum your one in a million with the way you listen, always giving encouragement and you never seem to give any negative thoughts on my views and give me so much love; Dad, we've had our ups and downs, but thanks for listening as well as your support; Alison, nobody could ask for more from a sister and being there when needed; Kate and Sarah my daughters who I'm very proud of and live their lives to the full, Christine you're always there for our children as well as me, and finally Clare for your support and encouragement.

Secondly for my many friends and business acquaintances who, if it wasn't for their trust and belief in what I have achieved in the past as well as what I hope to accomplish in the future, I wouldn't be publishing this book today, so special thanks must go to:

- Owen Richardson of McLaren Financial

- Martin Cooper of Total Results Ltd

- Brian Wardell

- Amanda Dixon for her marketing ideas and suggestions

- John Walton for finalising the book

- Rudi for his contributions for the cartoons at very short notice

- Wendy –Many thanks

- Gerard Wood

And many more individuals within the networking groups throughout the North East especially Network North, IPN Connect etc. You have all helped and encouraged in your special ways.

Contents

Introduction

This book is about trying to help others who are in debt now, or know in the future they are going to have financial problems and might think they have nowhere to turn. Hopefully, after reading this, you will know more about each individual way of resolving debt issues, or have more knowledge for when you talk to an advisor. By reading this you will not be bamboozled by the terminology of professionals and false promises made.

Personal circumstances will vary but from my experience debt occurs mainly for the following reasons: Redundancy, short time work, reduced hours on a temporary/permanent basis, maternity leave, a new job with less income, separation/divorce, illness, disability, bereavement, Self Employment, being a Director of a company, as well as many other worrying situations.

One of the first points I would like to make before you read this book, is to give you more of an understanding about financial issues. It's not the Bible about debt, (although I think it is), but a knowledge base for the average person about what some terminology/actions, means as well as the products and services available in simple language.

These are my personal views gained from my experience and background of helping people solve their financial problems.

Below you will find a very important statement which I want to emphasise very strongly and will be referring to quite often as you go through these pages.

Stop and think about the words! In one way or another, this will apply to you if you are having difficulties now, or worried you might have financial problems soon. You will then realise that you are not alone, there is always someone to listen and talk things over if you want to, but you have to make or take the first step, as people can't read your mind. Remember your family, experience has shown there is embarrassment if you are very young and don't want to tell your parents, brothers or sisters, uncle and aunties, or grandparents. There are also parents, pensioners as well as grandparents who come from the old school of thought who can be alone, afraid and embarrassed and don't want to tell their children. But remember the very good old fashioned saying "Blood is thicker than water". There are, of course, the individuals in this world that feel they are lonely, have no family and have no one in their lives. Please think of your friends, neighbours or someone you respect and trust who you could talk to in confidence. If all of these ideas have failed, there is always me and my staff who are there to listen, give you advice over the phone, by email (if you don't want to talk) or through the forum/video conferencing. However, primarily this book is not to advertise the company but to help and alleviate the stress levels you may be under by giving you knowledge and understanding.

SO PLEASE READ THE NEXT IMPORTANT SECTION IN BOLD.

So my statement:

Debt can be a very frightening and embarrassing issue, mentally as well as physically, making you feel subdued, depressed, lethargic, uncaring, wrapped up in your own issues, argumentative, feeling like the end of the world is near and probably distracting you from concentrating all your efforts on your work. If you are working with machinery you could cause an accident not just putting yourself in danger, but others as well.

It is a well known medical fact that 70% of stress within relationships, family and friends is based on money problems. I have stressed to my clients as well as speaking on stage, "you must talk"! It's easy to say, but taking the first step releases a whole lot of mental pressure knowing you have someone to talk to and the release you will feel will be so overwhelming you will become very emotional. This is why I have always had staff or myself on call to listen to existing and new clients about their worries and concerns for the future. Once again PLEASE TALK! Another saying many know is "a problem shared is a problem halved".

Just to reiterate the above bold statement:

You can go out for a drink with friends and family to your local pub and talk about your car having a problem, or your washing machine breaking down and someone will give you advice as to who they know who can help. Nobody goes into a pub and admits they have a debt problem, so they don't receive any help or advice and keep their worries to themselves, pretending to be OK.

I think this is where, in the past, I have been more of a social worker than a debt advisor, but I get immense pleasure as well as satisfaction helping before, as well as after, the problem has been solved. Even after years of not hearing from a client I will get an unexpected call out of the blue or a card at Christmas just to say "thank you", "you have changed my life" or "you will never be forgotten". There are many testimonials and examples within this book to share with others and I think it is important you read them, as it will give you an insight and might even resemble some or all of your own problems one way or another, proving that you are not alone or the only one.

Although I run a company called Action for Debt helping people with financial problems, this business wasn't started on a whim, thinking I could be better than my previous employer, or for the companies I worked for, advising on debt issues that I believed in and were right for the customer. No. It was set up because I believe there needs to be a wider option of choice for the individual. As the majority of the companies today only advise on 2 or 3 core products and turn people away who don't fit their criteria, my aim is to offer as many options as possible, as well as solving more complicated issues; I have experienced what many people are going through and understand your fear and trepidation. It's not through just reading books and thinking I'm an expert, the knowledge I have is way beyond that and the challenges I have gone through personally with Creditors, as well as going through the Courts helping others, gives me a wider and uniquely based foundation of problem solving. Going through the Courts for clients was a big step to take, arguing a defence against the legal profession, involving a house repossession, but my belief at what the lender was doing was wrong, unsympathetic and not allowing for the unexpected loss of job or illness or the reality that hits many people so frightened to talk and inform the lender.

Through having financial difficulties in the past, I have never had the opportunity to expand my business and fully utilise the vast knowledge I have in resolving problems for others. This is mainly due to my fees being far too low and, in some instances, doing work before getting the promised fee later!

In 1984 at the age of 24 and having built up a successful business employing over 10 staff, I had financial problems due to a large debt owed by a company who went into receivership. I had to close my business and sell all my vehicles, tools and equipment, as well as do the decent thing by finding jobs for my staff who were all trained to be the best. I'm proud to say, they all found employment.

In those very dark days with a wife, a two month old baby and having just moved into a newly built house, my thoughts turned to ending my life. I had an acute feeling that I was a failure and had been stupid for trusting customers. I was being threatened and intimidated by Creditors for payment. We had people knocking at the door day and night, non-stop phone calls as well having a deluge of threats via letters. We had concrete poured on our garden and a scaffolding pole thrown through our window while we were in the house.

If you believe you are suffering harassment with letters and phone calls now, believe me when I tell you that it is nothing compared to what the Creditors did in the 80s; they were more or less a law unto themselves. Today we have much improved protection and stronger rules relating to what a Creditor or Debt Collector can do. We have the Consumer Credit License as well as other authorities like the Office of Fair Trading, Financial Services Authority, Trading Standards, The Ministry of Justice and The Financial Ombudsman etc. We also have quite a good Court system that, in my opinion, is very fair minded in the event of having to defend these drastic steps. Although some lenders appointed representatives still break the rules, there are a lot more investigations regarding complaints about their behaviour and more fines and restrictions imposed.

When the above happened to me I had to seek urgent advice. This was like hitting a brick wall; my accountant had no knowledge or advice to give, the CAB were for the totally disadvantaged and were not experienced to help the Self Employed individual, and when I asked the Official Receivers for expert advice they declined my plea for help, saying they were sorry but they worked for the Crown. Even today you still don't get a straight answer to some questions you might require that are unusual from the norm and need answered before you take the steps of bankruptcy; they refer you to the help line, once again not always giving you an exact reply.

I learned more in 3 months by reading law, learning about Bankruptcy, County Court Judgment, issues with Bailiffs, as well as negotiating with Creditors in resolving my debt. In the 80s there were very few ways to solve financial issues. Fortunately, over the years, we now have new ways of helping people in difficulty. We have more structured Debt Management Plans, IVAs, Bankruptcy, DROs etc. which I will go into more detail later.

My aim is to try to help others, in plain speaking English, without the gobbledygook and the fears levied on the average person in the street. I hope this book will make it simple to understand the basics of what you might decide – as well as the product or service which is best for you and your family and not for others to dictate, who in the end are more interested in making money from you, in your desperate time of need.

You have to be aware of the large management fees as well as other professional fees that can be excessive and only line the pockets of these organisations. I would like to point out however, that you will have to seek professional advice for many of the options available. What I am trying to do is give you more knowledge so that you are not pressured into a product without knowing more about what you're signing or agreeing to, as you may be forced or rushed into signing a piece of paper thinking this is the only solution or way out of your debt problem.

Once again, as I said earlier, in the past I have run a few businesses, limited companies, as well as being a Financial Advisor specialising, at the time, in Pensions, Endowments and Mortgages. The knowledge I've gained gives me a far better understanding of the pressures you are under. My experience over the last 13 years in helping people with financial issues is based on working for many Debt Management Companies, (including Debt Collectors) as well as one of the best Insolvency Practitioners in the UK. I have won major contracts working on behalf of some of the leading National Debt Management and Insolvency Companies in the Country, completing the Statement of Affairs for Bankruptcy as well as stopping house repossessions with our unique financial pack for the Judges viewing, to decide whether an eviction should go ahead.

To date we have never lost a case!

We also have a department where we fight to get the lowest full and final settlements with Creditors. We have always been fair minded with our major customers by often referring a client back to them as our in depth questionnaire has occasionally found another alternative that wasn't recognised on the first interview.

Where I think I'm unique is wanting to know more about the client before giving advice. I need to know what the client wants for the future before looking at the current problem at hand. To give you a few ideas of what I'm talking about, let me give you a couple of examples:

We had a client who gave up his full time job to look after his mother, who unfortunately hadn't long to live. A company had suggested Bankruptcy and this was technically the right advice; however we found out he was going to receive a large inheritance when his mother passed away- and, let's be honest, our elderly have worked harder than we have ever done! They have provided for us and have saved in order to hopefully pass their possessions on to improve our standard of living and our future. If the client had gone bankrupt the Official Receivers would have appointed what is called a Trustee who would have added a fee of approximately £20,000 to his existing debt which the client would have had to pay from the inheritance. By doing a small Debt Management Plan for 6 months with his Creditors, we saved him the above fee. In fact we saved him more, as some Creditors accepted a lower amount as full and final settlement due to his circumstances and he didn't have to go bankrupt.

Another client was going to be offered a Directorship in the company he worked for. He was insisting he wanted to go bankrupt to get rid of his debt so he had a fresh start financially. We advised him that we were not prepared to help him down this route. He was stunned we were refusing work and thought the integrity of our advice was second to none. In the end he trusted our advice and entered an IVA. If he had gone ahead with bankruptcy, he would have had to resign as a Director and may not have been be able to be reinstated in the future, as his successor might have proved his worth. The company would probably have asked questions as to why he had to resign and this could have been rather embarrassing for him when his employers didn't have to know.

Maybe this is why I have never been able to expand the virtues of my knowledge in having offices all over the UK, as I have always kept my fees low to help the unfortunate. One of my biggest regrets to date has been not having the funds or finance in reserve for the bad times that we all have in our lives at one point or another. I personally went through an horrendous marriage break up, causing me financial problems in 2007. Then we had to move offices at short notice with all the added expense, as well as me being diagnosed with cancer which took a long time to recover from, mentally as well as physically. (As the statement above has mentioned, we never know what's round the corner). My belief, if I had had the funds, is I would have been a national success with the way I advise and train my staff, giving best advice as well as showing compassion to each individual, never classing someone as a number but as a person. That said, the banks have always been reluctant to lend, as they would lose out on my advice, one way or the other, as there's a good chance they would lose all or some of the money owed by clients.

I do feel strongly that many debt problems have been caused by the banks as well as finance houses and shops, insisting that their staff push more credit onto the general public. I know we should all take responsibility for our actions in taking loans and credit cards, but human instinct gets the better of us all and we don't look far enough into the future regarding our own job, family situation and finances. We think next week, next month or next year will be better, or the next bonus is due if we do this or do that. Remember I've been there and got the t-shirt!

(I didn't know at the time I was going to divorce or get cancer).

Again to give you some examples:

I've witnessed and so have you, those fantastic offers that sound too good to be true, where a car dealer advertises "You could have a brand new car for £99 deposit and £99 per month". The brain thinks "I can afford that and have a new car". In years past finance was typically over 2 to 5 years and the car was paid off and you had some value. Now lenders are extending these terms and what you've bought has no value at the end of the loan term, or there could possibly be a lump/balloon payment at the end of the agreement, costing more than the car is worth.

Another large issue has been the misinterpretation of taking out a loan where Payment Protection or life insurance was added, where the client had been told they would only get the loan if they accepted these expensive add-ons, or didn't know it had been added. This has often been the case even though there has been no medical or employment questions asked. I had a couple who borrowed £30,000 and a further £15,000 was added for PPI. One of the clients had a heart condition which wouldn't have been covered and the other was Self Employed – if they had tried to claim, the insurance company wouldn't have paid out. The further ironic issue was this loan was for 10 years and the protection cover was only for the first 5 years! We don't always read the small print, do we? We fought on behalf of the client a refund of the PPI which, when received, reduced their monthly payment to an affordable level and they didn't have to come to any financial arrangement.

I know we will never completely change the way we are sold products and services in this country, but my feelings are that we will always be wrongly sold a product or service when it's a commission orientated sale. I have a friend who works for a bank which has been taken over due to the banking crisis, and her contract of employment has been changed slightly. She works 20 hours a week and has been told that if she doesn't push all the products and services to the clients coming into the branch and doesn't put forward 86 potential sales per month, she will not be given a pay increase next year. Now just think of the number of phone calls and texts you get during the day and late into the evening and the times you go to the bank and are asked time and time again, "do you want this account"? Or "would you like a credit card" or "would you like house and life insurance" etc. It's an absolute disgrace!

Recently I went to my local Post Office, it was pouring with rain and people were queuing outside getting wet. All the assistants were asking each customer if they had life insurance, did they want a new type of bank account, were they going on holiday, did they want travel insurance or money exchanged. When I eventually got to the counter, highly annoyed, I asked why they couldn't ask these questions when there was less of a queue. The assistant's reply was "the Post Office made more money from those products than selling stamps, car tax or making benefit payments". Are these banks etc. not able to read our body language! We are a society which doesn't like to be pressured into things. We all know from adverts in the press, the internet, TV as well as shop windows where to go if we need or actually want something!

So where were we? I am very proud to have been on the Politics Show on BBC 1, The Money Box Programme on Radio 4 as well as on BBC local radio stations, giving advice as well as my opinions. I have been mentioned in the Times, the Guardian, the Daily Telegraph, The Mail as well as other local newspapers fighting the cause for individuals and the way some banks treat clients. I have been asked at many business network meetings to talk about debt and have helped many owner businesses and individuals discreetly, sometimes by just listening to their problems and suggesting an action to take.

Many work colleagues, friends and relatives have said I should write a book about what I have gone through including my own personal experiences in life. I believe this would be a boring subject and feel nobody would be interested. In fact, people would think it unbelievable, invented, a fabrication and would be made into the next comedy sketch if I went into depth sounding like a deranged individual seeking sympathy!

So this book is intended to go through the following in more basic detail, ending up with some examples to show possible ways and the consequences of those actions.

I would like at this stage to mention that in the near future I will have a debt advice line as well as an internet question and answer forum, as well as video conferencing giving advice which will be on a membership basis. Clients will pay a small fee to gain access to ask as many questions over a 1 month period for the advice they need. The web address as well as the phone numbers and how it works are at the end of this book. One thing I will guarantee – there is no premium rate telephone number!

Finally I have a personal and proud saying:

"If I can't help, nobody can".

So we will discuss in the next few chapters, hopefully, giving you the advice on the basis of each heading, as well as sub-heading within, giving you an understanding of the different avenues of help, the process, the terminology and the time frame that may be for your particular financial situation. Please note this is basic information, my words and thoughts and probably some professional organisations will not be entirely happy with what I have to say. However at least a large percentage of the population will be more informed and satisfied and hopefully this will alleviate some of the fears and concerns regarding future decisions.

I have to emphasise PLEASE READ ALL THE SECTIONS before you think you know a certain percentage of everything. Decide which way may be best for you and remember, think about the future not just the financial problem at the present time. To reiterate, if you are currently unemployed but believe within 6 months you will find a job and be earning £30,000 please THINK before you act on the product and READ ON for further advice.

Finally whatever you do, please don't lie or leave a Creditor out, you can, or will, be found out and this will have serious repercussions. You will not have read the small print in the majority of credit agreements; most have a clause saying the Creditor, at times, can review the credit agreement when they have concerns or on a regular basis determined by the bank. Do you remember the news a few years ago where Barclaycard as well as Egg and other lenders reduced credit limits or cancelled cards altogether? There was uproar for many, as some hadn't used their cards for months or even years and had the facility stopped, (one wonders if this was because the bank wasn't making any money). If you enter an IVA or a DMP they may (but it is very unusual) just look at your credit file and see if what you have declared as all your Creditors really is a complete list, to ensure you haven't kept one out for some specific reason. If this was found, then you are technically making a lender what's called a preferred Creditor which is wrong and further legal action could be taken.

We will touch on the following and in the same order. The first section is background information on some of my personal beliefs on the free services as well as some of the meanings and consequences of some the main threats you may come across. The next section is to explain some of the products and services that are available, but remember these are not all of them.

Please note regarding three specific areas. If you live in Scotland, the process of going Bankrupt is different to England, Wales and Northern Ireland and you can't do an IVA as such, as they have what's called a Trust Deed. In Northern Ireland the process of going Bankrupt is different to the UK. These slight differences are also explained in separate headings. All will be revealed.

CAB (Citizens Advice Bureau)

Although this service is a charity which is financed predominantly by the banks and the government, I have to say I don't have much faith in them. I feel the staff are not adequately trained and don't offer many of the services that need to be offered in today's economic and financial climate. It has only been in this last year or so that the CAB has started to suggest bankruptcy and IVAs. Instead, they seem to be content in sending letters to Creditors offering minimal sums of money as low as a £1 per Creditor, when the client can be £1,000s in debt, damaging their credit history for many years in the future, as well as having Creditors demanding more money and still contacting the clients. There is, in my opinion, a further fundamental problem – although they arrange your minimum payment, it is up to you to pay each individual Creditor on time yourself. If you then miss a payment for whatever reason, they are not happy to help you a second time to renegotiate.

One of my previous members of staff went to work for this charity and was *so* embarrassed at the training she was given. Supposedly staff have approximately one week's training to gain basic knowledge of rent arrears, mortgage problems, repossession, debt issues, divorce, separation as well as rights on certain issues of employment, family law and child safety matters to mention a few.

You will also find that it is normal to book an appointment, sometimes up to 3 weeks in advance and they only allow approximately 10/20 minutes for a meeting. For an individual to have the courage to pick up the phone, admit to having a debt problem and then be told to wait weeks for an appointment is an absolute disgrace and prolongs the agony for a solution. My staff receive a full week of training, just on debt alone, and have to take 20/30 scenarios/tests before they are allowed to give advice!

How any institution can give best advice in 20/30 minutes is beyond my comprehension when it comes to financial matters. Many CAB offices are not open 5 days a week and are rarely open to the public at 9am or after 5pm. The average opening hours per day is 4/5 hours, although most are open for only part days per week and I haven't known them to be open at weekends or after hours on a regular basis.

There is no thought for the client who has to take time off work, without pay, or take valuable holiday to see them and travel miles to get there. As this book was written during 2010 to give you a current example, Sunderland, with a population larger than Newcastle upon Tyne, only has one office within the local County Court building in the City.

The staff are there to mainly give advice on what to say at a hearing on the day in front of a Judge – this could be for house repossessions, family issues as well other debt issues. They are open the same hours as the Court which is 10am-4pm, with an hour to an hour and a half for lunch (4 and a half working hours a day!)

The remaining public have to travel to a town called Chester le Street which is over 10 miles away from the North East end of the City. This is hardly what I would consider to be a great effective service.

Sorry to say but I was threatened with legal action a few years ago by the CAB. I had helped a reclusive client who had gained so much weight through stress that he couldn't get out of his apartment. I gave him advice (he was not working), he had debts in the region of £50,000 and he chose to go bankrupt. Once he had gone through the process, he dramatically lost weight and his doctor was amazed. After being informed by his niece of what we had done, he contacted me and said I should send leaflets to all the surgeries in the North East. I did this and didn't suggest in any way on our leaflet that everything was free, but we offered a free home consultation giving the options available. Within two weeks we got a letter from the Newcastle CAB demanding we withdraw our leaflets as we didn't inform them we charged a fee and we were a Debt Management Company. We have never been a DMP company. We have always been Debt Counsellors. We were threatened with legal action and I returned the threat via a counter claim for defamation of character. I had great satisfaction to receive a two lined letter of apology which I keep on file to this day. It is sad to think the head of the CAB for the North East at the time felt he was superior in giving best advice. At the time of this friction, we exposed and named clients, as well as the advisors, with what they had done to some unfortunate people like promising to go to Court to help a couple stop their house from repossession. The original advisor left the CAB and the new member of staff who took over the case said she would attend Court with them. She didn't turn up and the clients lost their home. As far as we are concerned it was the first hearing for repossession and if they had been represented, the Judge would not have followed through with the eviction.

In another case, a gentleman who was widowed had a house with no Mortgage valued at £110,000 had debts of £20,000 and was told to sell his house. His minimum monthly payment to Creditors was £400 per month; we suggested a DMP at £150 per month or to look at remortgaging his house at a lower interest rate at £116 per month and advising him, if he had further lump sums, to pay the loan off as fast as possible. These at the time were just some of the many horror stories we heard about and it's a pity the manager didn't put more effort into training and reorganising staff and office opening hours in those days, but there again they haven't changed to date.

As far as I am concerned there have to be better ways to help clients than offer an insulting minimum £1, £5 etc to each Creditor where the client will pay forever. I don't want to degrade people with my next statement, but this service is for the unemployed as well as the extremely low paid and people who are mainly on very basic pensions or benefits. If you are Self Employed, forget it! Remember this is just my personal view.

CCCS (Consumer Credit Counselling Service)

Far better than the CAB, a free service which has staff at hand most days from 8am-8pm so you can contact them in the evenings without having time off work. Their staff are far more caring or it sounds that way to me, and have a lot more time to listen to your plight. The main problem is that all discussions are on the telephone and not face to face, although we know being a National organisation this is not possible. They don't offer all the options available that we would look at on a problem solving basis. Again, it's only over the last few years that they have advised on bankruptcy and IVAs. One of the good things with the CCCS is that they run their own DMPs with no management fee, they pay all your Creditors from the monthly payment you make and they keep you informed by sending a statement as to what your balance is. We have, however, noticed some Creditors have not frozen the interest or still charge for late payment, thus defeating the object i.e. instead of reducing your balance it could be increasing (I think the Creditors who do this should be named and shamed when they know the client has financial problems). But in the main the CCCS are a very good organisation.

Contact Details:

Consumer Credit Counselling Service
Wade House
Merrion Centre
Leeds
LS2 8NG

Opening hours are: 8am – 8pm

Website: www.cccs.co.uk

Tel: 0800 1381111

Pay Plan

The same good service as the CCCS and seem to be more for the professional bodies such as the Police Force, NHS, and Civil Service etc. The problem once again is that they do not offer all the far reaching options required in my opinion, but still a very professional free service. They do their own in house Debt Management Plans without charging a fee. Once again they are open late in the evenings.

Contact Details:

Payplan Ltd.
Kempton House
Dysart Road
Grantham
Lincolnshire
NG31 7LE

Opening Hours are: 8am – 8pm

Website: www.payplan.com

Tel: 0800 280 2816

The Family Income Survey

Believe it or not there is certain expenditure allowed per person within the household. It is set and based on being the acceptable minimum level to live on. Most Creditors and Debt Agencies know about this and are supposed to work from these amounts; unfortunately this is not the case and you have to understand staff working for Lenders and Creditors are under a lot of pressure and receive bonus when they get you to pay more. If you contact them and offer to pay a Creditor say £30 per month, they will reply saying it's unacceptable and ask for double. This is how they are trained and you have to be firm with your offer. Please don't be intimidated to pay more than you can afford as once you have offered a sum and in the future you fail and miss payments, they have a record and evidence to take further action.

Sorry forgot to take into account five week months

Financial Expenditure

With the many different areas of resolving debt issues like IVAs, DMPs, Bankruptcy and trying to negotiate yourself an agreement, it can be very difficult, due to the pressure from Creditors, to pay more than you can afford. There are different expenditures limits allowed depending on the product you decide on. What you have to be very careful of is working out your exact monthly expenditure; I hope you read the last sentence, **"exact monthly expenditure"**.

What I mean by this is someone might say I spend £20 per week on petrol and say that's £80 per month; it's not, its £86.60 per month. To expand on this, whatever your weekly amount is, whether its wages, school activities, school meals etc you have to do a calculation. Multiply the weekly payment by 4.33 and this is the monthly sum to average 5 week months etc. Remember if you're paid wages, Tax Credits etc by 4 weekly, you need to divide the amount by 4 and multiply by 4.33 to get your monthly income correct. If you pay something annually, like car insurance, vehicle recovery, union fees, of course it's divide by 12 and finally regarding being Self Employed, remember your National Insurance Contribution as well as your personal tax liabilities to pay at the end of your financial year; they have to be allowed within the expenditure.

Many DMP companies don't ask these questions when completing the paperwork and this can be difficult when you have to say, "Sorry Creditors I can't pay this month's payment, I have a tax bill".

Unfortunately some expenditure is frowned upon and questions will be asked; they include large club memberships like golf and fitness centres or expenditure for stabling horses, having many pets or children's extra expenditure from the norm like travelling the country doing Irish dancing/Judo/Football competitions etc. I'm not saying these will be refused, but they will need to be explained. Smoking is another issue Creditors don't allow or frown upon; I know what you're going to say "I need to smoke I can't give up with all this stress"; and finally drugs for self use; believe it or not, this is becoming more of a frequent question as well as an issue in today's society.

You might think this is penny pinching but just look at this very limited example, as to what you are short changing yourself in terms of expenditure based on a family of four:

	Weekly	4 Weekly	Monthly
Fuel	£20	£80	£86.60
Food	£110	£440	£476.30
School meals	£20	£80	£86.60
Electric	£15	£60	£64.95
Gas	£20	£80	£86.60
Rent	£80	£320	£346.40
Parking	£10	£40	£43.30
Clothing	£10	£40	£43.30
Council Tax	£30	£120	£129.90
TOTAL	**£315**	**£1260**	**£1363.95**

As you can see just on the items above, there is a difference of **£103.95** between the 4 weekly and monthly calculations so beware, as once you have agreed with Creditors an amount to pay each month there is no going back saying you have made a mistake and you can't afford the monthly commitment.

Debt Collection Agencies

When a lender has failed to come to an arrangement with you directly to resolve the debt you owe, the bank will usually instruct a debt collection agency to try to get you to come to an arrangement. Can I point out at this stage that these companies earn on average 30% of the debt. Sometimes lenders will give the debt to a few agencies at the same time and it's then a race to contact you to get an agreed repayment plan put in place. Once you have made an arrangement with one of these companies, they inform the lender and the remaining agents are told to stop. Although they have a job to do these collectors are trained to be quite intimidating and can be quite frightening on the phone as well as by letter and some do have agents who visit your home, although there are few that actually have the resources. (In fact many door collectors are Self employed agents and get a commission on what they collect and this can be as much as 20%).

There is one certain company in Scotland (who I would love to name) who has the gall to demand you contact family and friends to get the money or they threaten they will keep ringing every day until you pay. (They have been fined due to the number of complaints made against them) but it can and does happen; please note they are not Bailiffs and have no power other than to ask you to pay. They try to get you to make a commitment by asking you to complete an Income & Expenditure statement, but this cannot be forced upon you (although we would suggest it would help your situation) unless through a Court Order. You will often get letters on a daily basis from the same company demanding the full amount or demand that you ring them without fail or further action will be taken.

Many of these sinister looking letters are attempts to get you to act and if you ring them they will ask for payment straight away. In most cases these companies can threaten Court action but don't or can't implement as this is not usually their job. When you get a letter, have a look to see if they mention they are Solicitors at the top or bottom of the page. Most are not, and when they fail to get an agreement your file is returned to the lender, it could be sent to a solicitor for further action or the whole process could start all over again with another agency.

Companies Who Buy Debt

This is becoming the new way to collect debt. After a certain amount of time, when the lenders have given up hope of getting their money back, the bank sells the debt to another company. If this happens you should be notified by the bank as well as by the new owner of the debt. Take advice as soon as possible, especially if you own your own home or have property or land elsewhere. This is only a suggestive idea or theory, but a company will buy let's say £4 million pounds worth of debt from a bank for £1 million. They get the whole client file and usually the agreement. Once they have these, there on a race against time to get money as fast as possible to pay off the debt they paid to buy the debt so as to move into profitability.

To do this they look through the files for anyone who owns a house and chase these debts first. If you don't come to an agreement, they will take legal action by way of a County Court Judgment then apply for a Charging Order on the property. It has been known, if there was mass equity, to go further by applying for what's called a Forced Sale, or making you Bankrupt, thus releasing monies from the estate. Please beware and take advice as soon as you get this type of letter. In some circumstances you have to look at options that might delay these actions, such as asking for a copy of the credit agreement, which some can't find, and looking to see if it could be unenforceable, or you could look at an Interim Order, Time Out Order as well as an IVA. Be careful, these companies are more ruthless in demanding what's owed.

County Court Judgments (CCJs)

I think everyone knows what these are, but let's explain. When you don't pay your agreement on time or come to an arrangement, the Creditor can apply to the Court for the full balance to be paid. When this action has been instigated, you are sent notice and you have to complete an income and expenditure statement telling the Courts how much you can afford to pay. It then goes in front of a Judge and he usually makes the order as he thinks fit (So remember, put full expenditure down as well as why you can't pay more, explaining as much as possible and use additional paper, don't think you have to put everything into the limited space available). If you ignore this or don't ask to have a hearing to explain further your predicament or reasons for non-payment, then the Judge will order in favour of the plaintiff/creditor. This is then a Court Order that you must comply with or you could have further action taken against you, for instance, Attachment of Earnings, Charging Order (if you have property) or visits to your home from a Court Bailiff.

Many people just think "Oh well I have a CCJ now", but you should take this more seriously. Some creditors don't take further action after lodging such a claim, although others will, but this is the biggest damage you can do to your credit history apart from going bankrupt. Please also note that it stays on your credit file even though you might have paid the debt off. Your file will show you've had one and it will stay for 6 years. If you pay a CCJ within the time allowed (14 days) this will not show on your credit file; however if you do pay later than allowed, I would advise you ask for a certificate of satisfaction from the creditor/court and send this to the credit reference agencies to make sure this correction is noted. This will go some way to improving your credit score.

If the Creditor is owed a large amount of money and thinks you have equity or income to pay the money that's claimed, the next step could be to issue you with a Statutory Demand. These are very serious and you need to see the section below.

Note: Some very large organisations are using the bulk processing system in Northampton to issue CCJs on line; please be aware that it can take up to 5/7 days for the paperwork to be processed and sent by post, leaving you a very limited time frame to pay or reply before the deadline.

Statutory Demands

These demands are more serious than a County Court Judgment and you don't have to have a CCJ before receiving one. In general you have 18 days to pay the debt, or reply within the same period with your objections and why you do not agree with this action; it is advised that you also apply to the Court for it to be set aside. If you don't pay or ignore this request, the Creditor can start proceedings to make you bankrupt (or if a limited company, have it wound up). Usually this type of demand is served upon you by hand by what's called a Process Server; if this is not possible, it can be posted or put through your letter box classing it as substituted service. A server has to do a Statement of Truth that he has complied under the rules as this is part of the evidence for the future petition. You must act very fast as the Creditor after this period of time can start proceedings anytime in the future, as there is no expiry time limit to make you Bankrupt. You can't really appeal against this action after the time limit of 21 days, unless you can prove you never received it, were working away, on holiday or had moved house etc. Although the Bankruptcy petition would still have to be heard in front of a judge, this would be your final chance of delaying the action, objecting or offering a significant payment within a very short period of time.

Pressure from Charging Orders can keep you locked into long term misery with no escape.

Charging Orders

These are usually asked for by a Creditor after a County Court Judgment has failed to make you pay. This could be because you have not kept up with the order regarding the payment demanded, or you ignored it or didn't return the papers required (or never received them as they are sent by standard post). Some Creditors would then apply to the Court for a Charging Order which means the debt is secured against your property. This is becoming more common, although you can defend this on what I would say is a fine line and an argument against this action that you never signed an agreement that said your home was at risk and what you have paid up to the time of the difficulties the bank charged a higher interest rate for taking the risk of lending unsecured. It would be up to a Judge to decide on this argument, but it has been won in the past. You have to be aware interest can continually be added at a set rate until the debt has been settled.

Administration Orders

These orders, although very rare nowadays, are a process whereby you visit the Court. It's free to do and you are protected from your Creditors. It gives you a temporary amount of time to put your finances in order. To qualify for this type of order, you must have no more than £5,000 of debt, owe more than one Creditor, and have at least one County Court Judgment against you. Once again these are for people on low income and in rented accommodation and you should also look at a DRO.

Harassment From Creditors

As we are going through the different areas that cause stress and the constant harassment from phone calls, letters and knocks on the doors by banks, debt collectors, bailiffs etc, although they threaten, a lot don't take the matter any further, although I think in the future this could increase. In the main it's words and threats, yes you might be threatened or have a CCJ or a bailiff at your door, but what else can they do if you are in rented accommodation? When you read the following, please take note as to what powers they have. What I would suggest if Creditors are constantly ringing the house or mobile and pestering you, would be to ring your supplier and ask to change the number and go ex-directory. This could alleviate quite a lot of the stress of picking up the phone wondering if its family, friends, the lender or debt collector.

I've been phoned
six times a day can
I complain?

Complaining About Creditors/Debt Agencies/Collectors

There are many laws which cover certain harassment from Creditors and although very rare, can instigate a Criminal Offence. If they are found to ring constantly, calling at your home as well as workplace or anti-social hours it could constitute harassment. I have known banks to call up to 8 times a day and this can be very distressing.

To complain about a Creditor or Debt Agency you must gather evidence as to when they have telephoned or called at your home or place of work. This can be difficult as many banks and debt collectors use withheld numbers. All we can suggest is that you ring your phone provider again and tell them you don't want withheld numbers ringing you. The Creditor will then have to use a number you can identify. This will let you know who is calling. Unfortunately, another problem is some debt collectors and banks use a computer system that allows them to ring many clients at the same time and as soon as someone answers the phone the other lines go dead when you pick up the phone.

You can complain. The first point of call is in writing to the company as well as the Office of Fair Trading, sending them copies of letters sent and diarise all actions that have occurred. It can be a long process though; if you had 3 to 4 weeks of logged calls, I think this would be enough justification, but this is all you can do and while an investigation is carried out many calls will or should stop. You must have the information to support how many instances you've had, what time of the day and what was said, preferably getting the name of the person you have talked to on each conversation. We do know that some lenders and debt agencies don't even collate what you've said; for instance if a partner was ill, in hospital or there was a more significant problem, and ring you an hour later or the next day.

Bailiffs

This is a frightening area whereby I've had clients take their lives because of the stress due to the personal embarrassment or the thought of having all their possessions taken, as well as having the property broken into in front of the neighbours. THIS IS VERY RARE! First of all bailiffs don't have the power to take everything (see below) and the only time a door might be forced is when a house is being repossessed where a County Court bailiff would be in attendance or when a walking possession is held, although, once again, this is rare unless what has been levied is an expensive non essential item. (See section below on this).

Let's try to break down the difference between the three main types of bailiffs as well as what they can do. **Please remember that you do not have to allow them into your property. A bailiff cannot force his/her way into your house, and he/she has to use what's called peaceful means.**

Council rent and Council Tax Bailiffs. (Private Bailiffs)

These are usually private bailiffs under contract to Councils or Magistrate who have an order to recover arrears for Council tax and rent, parking fines and traffic and other related fines etc. Note: Magistrates' Orders are not County Court Judgments and are not recorded on your personal credit file.

These bailiffs cannot break into your property and take possessions unless you have allowed access previously. They are allowed to put what's called a Levy or a Walking Possession Agreement on goods; if the bailiff has done this, he would ask you to sign a declaration that he has control of the items and you agree not to remove or sell the goods as technically the bailiff owns them until discharged from the security. Usually, when a bailiff has this on record he would allow a limited time to pay the outstanding balance and if you don't, the bailiff can break in and take what was listed, although experience shows that this is quite rare depending on the area. Please note that for every visit, they can charge and there doesn't seem to be a set amount.

The main thing to bear in mind is these bailiffs cannot threaten you, put their foot in the door to stop you closing it and cannot break in unless they have been in before. They can however gain entry if a door is unlocked or a window is left open, as this is called peaceful means of entry.

Please note, however, if you have a vehicle outside your house in your name, they can take it after informing you they have levied. Usually they contact DVLC and do an HPI check to see who the owner is and if it has hire purchase, contract hire, personal contract hire or any other finance secured on the vehicle, they cannot remove it. They cannot, or shall we say they shouldn't, take a vehicle that helps you to get to work or you are self employed as this is classed as tools of the trade.

If you ever have Council debt, please contact your main County Hall and talk to someone high up to discuss your personal situation. If it's a fine, contact your local Magistrates' Court and ask for time to pay or demand a hearing in front of a Magistrate to explain your predicament.

If a bailiff, after a certain amount of time, does not resolve the financial debt owed, it usually goes back to the plaintiff and a decision will be made on the next legal steps to take. Again please talk to them, some will listen.

County Court Bailiffs

These types of bailiffs are far easier to deal with and most are quite pleasant to talk to, although they still have a job to do in recovering the debt owed. They have to inform you in writing that they are going to attend your premises, but don't have to give a time. The same issues apply regarding the levying/walking possession on goods, but let's say they are not as arrogant in the way they talk to you and try to help, suggesting ideas to resolve the situation.

This could be to apply to the Court for a N244, (there is usually a fee to pay of approximately £65 unless you are on certain benefits), to ask for the warrant to be suspended/ stay of execution. Usually you would have to go to the Court and make an appointment to see a Judge to explain your reasons. The bailiff also has discretion as well as being able to talk to the Creditor to arrange further time, if he thinks there is a genuine case to solve the issue.

High Court/ Sheriffs Officer/Bailiffs

The High Court/Supreme Court is based in the Royal Courts of Justice in London and in many large towns. They are mainly used for larger debts over £25,000 although debts over £15,000 that are not regulated by the Consumer Act of 1974 can also be included. When a claim is pursued in the above Court, a High Court bailiff is instructed to enforce the debt. They can move more quickly as they don't have to inform you by letter they are coming to visit, whereas a County Court Bailiff does. Although they are more powerful and have a job to do, once again, in general, they can be easier to talk to, just like a County Court Bailiff.

What can Bailiffs take from the home?

I personally believe there should be a standard list of what a bailiff can take from your home or business, but believe it or not, there isn't one. It is up to the individual bailiff as to what they class as non-essentials items. Once again there are no set rules on this area. All I will say is why take something that won't gain any money at auction? Goods sold now have restrictions; before selling some electrical appliances they have to be checked, and there are auctioneers fees to pay for any goods sold and with the financial climate of today, prices are falling drastically. For instance, a used TV will only sell for about £35. Bailiffs can't take clothes and furniture or household provisions that are necessary for basic domestic needs for you and family members. Once again, there is no absolute rule, but in the main they have to leave you something to sit on for each person in the household and leave you something to cook on and with. They are not supposed to take what's called tools of the trade for your employed work or vocation, so needing your car to get to work as well as use of computers are not supposed to be taken, especially when you're Self Employed. There are certain private bailiffs, who I have no respect for and will not mention their names, just to emphasise, you have to be quite tough with these people and I would call the Police and get witnesses if there were any raised voices or threats or continuous banging on doors and windows.

How to stop actions of a bailiff?

As previously stated, County Court bailiffs are quite helpful, please respect them and they will try to help. If it is the private bailiff element there is no real regulatory body with decent power to complain to, all I can say is plead with the Creditor. Some Councils will help, others won't, and can also be as arrogant as the bailiffs in saying you have had your chances to pay and it is out of their hands. This is rubbish. They gave the order and it's their responsibility to be caring and listen to your plight. I would advise you get your local MP or local Councillor to take up your plea.

In the end, if you don't let them into your property, the debt is returned to the Council to decide on further action and this could be another hearing in Court to try to impose further fines or frightening you with the extreme of imprisonment. What you will have is a chance at the hearing to explain your reasons as to why you haven't paid, and usually you're given further time to make payment.

Although it is easy for me to write and advise about bailiffs, I had an elderly couple who thought they were doing the honourable act by allowing them into their home to talk instead of on the doorstep; they didn't understand what a Walking Possession was and goods were Levied.

Unfortunately they allowed other bailiffs for another debt to Levy on the same goods which of course is not allowed. (As I keep referring back to my statement, the elderly are sometimes embarrassed to talk). I know it took tremendous courage for them to pick up the phone for advice and although I tried to stop the bailiff actions, begging them under the circumstances, they refused.

Following this, I talked to the couple sympathetically and finally persuaded them to allow me to talk to family and explain their predicament. I explained the problem, but also informed them of other substantial debts they had and asked if they had monies available. As this was impossible, I suggested that, under the circumstances, maybe Bankruptcy might be the only option. This was agreed and after much debate, we completed the paperwork for Court. With great sadness I was informed by the family that the elderly gentlemen had taken his life as he couldn't face the embarrassment or humiliation. My heart sank when I was told the news and my immediate reaction was to question my own advice and wonder could I have come to another solution, but this was not the case. The family rang me to see if I was ok as they knew I was so upset, but also acknowledged that my advice was correct and the widow went bankrupt a few weeks later.

I will never forget what those bailiffs did to this couple and I hope they can live with their intimidating actions. (Please note these were private bailiffs)

Times Bailiffs can visit you

Basically, bailiffs can call during the day or night; the majority work from 8am-8pm Monday to Saturday. In general at Christmas the majority of Court bailiffs don't visit from about the 22 December to approximately the

4th January, but there are no real guidelines for private bailiffs!

Fees Bailiffs Charge

There seems to be some confusion as to what the standard charges are for private bailiffs for each visit they make. We have experience of anything from £15 to £70 per visit, and this can be added to the amount outstanding. Once again, some of these bailiffs are very sneaky in how they add fees to the debt and this is from my personal experience.

I moved house and forgot to notify DVLA until 18 months after I moved. When I finally informed them, within a week I received a letter from Hartlepool Magistrates demanding I pay a fine for non-disclosure of naming the driver for a speeding camera offence (me). I tried to plead my situation and explained I had paid for the redirection of all my mail but hadn't received the summons, but agreed to pay within the next week as it was too old to contest or defend.

48 hours later I was parked up the road from my house waiting for an employee to give her a lift to the office; as she entered the vehicle, she asked if I was waiting for a parcel as a van was outside my property. As we watched, a male driver went up to my front door, didn't knock, and put an envelope through my letter box and drove off. We noted the registration of the vehicle and as I was curious with my partner being in the house, I stopped to see what it was and yes you guessed it, a bailiff had left a letter saying he had called, that we weren't, in, and he had charged a fee of £70 for the visit. I complained in writing to the Magistrate's Court as well as the bailiff's head office. Although I received acknowledgment from the Court, I had no such luck with the bailiffs when I tried to

talk to them; unfortunately the employee was very rude, unhelpful and was kind enough to put the phone down on me. I sent a further letter of complaint, enclosing a cheque for the fine, informing them not to cash it unless the bailiff fee was written off, as I would take things further and demand a hearing. They cashed the cheque and have not been in touch for the visit charged.

Complaining about a Bailiff:

In the first instance, you should complain to the person who instructed the bailiff and inform them of your complaint and demand that they investigate. You have to remember the Creditors will have heard all the excuses under the sun, and usually side with the bailiffs unless you have explicit evidence of what they have done and hopefully have witnesses. You can also make a complaint to the main trade associations, The Certificated Bailiffs Association (CBA), or the Association of Civil Enforcement Agencies (ACEA). As you can see by the names, they are associations and I haven't heard many direct orders or large fines handed out against many bailiffs whether independent or major companies. Again, in my opinion, it seems to be an internal investigation with a slap on the hand and told not to do it again.

Addresses:

The Certificated Bailiffs Association
C/O Ridgefield House, 14 John Dalton Street, Manchester M2 6JR

Association of Civil Enforcement Agencies
Chesham House, 150 Regent Street, London W1R 5FA

Credit Reference Agencies

Nowadays, I think it is very important that you check your personal details regularly; however you should use more than just one company as I have personally found many agreements I've had in the past don't show all my information. As to reading your credit file, it takes a little getting used to with all the additional information they have added, for the better I may add, but it can be confusing for the average person to understand. I would suggest you look at your file on a 3/6 monthly basis, especially if you have moved house, or you have moved to different properties on a regular basis, until you found somewhere more secure. I come across many clients who find loans and credit cards, especially catalogues which have been registered against them, but can be very hard to prove otherwise, so beware.

Equifax PLC
P.O. Box 1140 Bradford BD1 5US

Opening Hours: 9am – 5pm Monday to Friday

Web Address: www.equifax.co.uk

Tel: 0844 3350550

Experian
PO BOX 7710, Nottingham, NG80 7WE

Opening Hours: Monday to Friday 8am to 7pm, and Saturday 8am to 4pm

Web Address: www.experian.co.uk

Tel: 0844 481 0800

Call Credit Ltd
One Park Lane Leeds LS3 1EP

Opening Hours: 8am – 6pm Monday to Friday

Web Address: www.callcreditcheck.co.uk

Tel: 0113 2441555

Talking To Creditors in More Positive Ways

You have been told and read about it, all I can do is confirm the same statements. As soon as you foresee you're going to have problems, talk to your lender. You will find quite a few finance institutions have changed drastically, especially the High Street banks who will tell you they don't have the power to accept your offer and can't discuss in house and tell you to ring the head office to resolve your predicament.

Once again the personal touch with your local Bank Manager has gone; they are puppets and their job is to manage the staff in branch and push targets. A long time ago, a Bank Manager had discretion; you were able to talk to them and they could make decisions based on your body language, as well as having local knowledge of the area regarding a local business making redundancies or short term working practices due to weather, a delay in a large order etc. They were far more sympathetic and made humane judgments. All I would advise is to tell them your situation, offer them what you can and leave it at that (See section on banks as well bank accounts)

Banks

I am going to make another statement here and it's blunt and a lot of you are going to have to wake up to the fact. Finance companies are tightening their criteria on who they're going to lend to and this won't change for the next 5 years in my opinion.

High Street banks have changed; most Managers and their staff have very little authority to say yes to an increase in your overdraft, loan or credit card application. They now have to input your details on a computer and it says yes or no to your request. Managers are now in branches to manage staff and have less responsibility for looking after the customers who pay their wages!

I know what you're going to say, "My Bank has been very good to me" and "I've had no problems with them "I have a good job", "they wouldn't refuse me", "I've been with them for years". Please don't be lulled into a false sense of security.

OF COURSE YOU HAVEN'T! YOU'VE NEVER HAD TO ASK THEM FOR HELP WHEN YOU'VE HAD FINANCIAL PROBLEMS IN RECENT TIMES!

The banks are happy when you are paying interest and not causing any problems with missed payments, going overdrawn, bouncing cheques etc. Tell me this; how can a friend of mine with perfect credit history and a fantastic job be refused a Mortgage? In the days of the 80s a common income multiple for affording Mortgages was three times one wage and one of the other, or two and a half times joint income, whichever the greater. (He was refused on two times his income) In all areas of lending for personal loans, overdrafts and credit cards etc. decision making has changed drastically!

My experience is that this is one of the most fundamental areas that start a lot of financial problems, when the bank says NO to you for an extension on an overdraft or consolidating loans or renewing one for whatever reason. You will go into panic mode, your internal stress levels will soar and the pressure will build internally, knowing you might have problems if you go past your overdraft or can't make the next loan repayment on time.

All I am going to say is, if you think you are going to have any financial problems in the foreseeable future or you're on the verge of this, **please open a new bank account straight away with one you have no debts with.** (So if you have a Barclaycard, don't go with Barclays bank). **Keep this new account as a standby or emergency.**

The reason for this is when you apply for a new bank account, they will do a credit check and it will show all the credit agreements you have as well as missed payments, your overdraft limit at your existing bank and if you have exceeded it. If you have, then you will have limited choice on what another bank will accept or the type of account offered. (Note if you're thinking of going bankrupt please read the section regarding bank accounts beforehand)

You may ask why do this? Just to give another example: If you have an overdraft and your facility is say £1,000 and your income is £1,200 per month then you know you have to tighten your belt. (You are continually living in an overdraft) However let's say you've had to take a pay cut or another common problem, your benefits are reduced. Once you miss a payment or go overdrawn, the bank will start taking more interest about the activity of your account and may put pressure on you by reducing your overdraft facility. Suddenly your wages/income is reduced to say £800 and the bank wants to reduce your overdraft by £100 per month or close it altogether. (In the small print many only have to give 14 days' notice). If this happens, well you know the answer; your wages go in and you have no money to live on as the bank has swallowed your income to pay the overdraft. This is why you need a new account on standby so that if this threat is made, you can notify your employer as well as benefit departments to have your income paid into the new account putting you in control of your own money. You can then come to an arrangement with your old bank on your terms and not theirs. (Remember stay in the black, not in the red)

Pressure from negative equity and secured loans can keep you locked into misery for years with no escape.

Mortgage/Secured Loan Problems

I think everybody knows you must talk to your Mortgage and Secured lender as soon as you think you are going to have problems. It's very important for many reasons especially if you haven't missed a payment, as the lender can help and offer more options to the situation you're in.

If you're not in arrears your lender (Mortgages mainly) will listen to you more favourably and may offer certain options to relieve the pressure. You can ask for a payment holiday which could be up to 6 months in some cases and if your Mortgage is on a repayment basis, you could ask for the payments to be reduced to interest only where there would be significant savings to help with your monthly budget.

We have to tell you it's rare if you have missed a payment with your Mortgage provider that they will allow you to change to the above unless you have caught up the arrears owed. We know you're not paying anything off the Mortgage balance when on interest only, but needs must prevail over the norm, as in keeping a roof over your family. When your financial situation recovers, you can change back to a repayment plan. (Note a lender can charge a fee for doing this and usually adds this to the balance of the loan – on average about £100).

Unfortunately Secured Loans invariably won't allow you to change to interest only. Why this is? I can't see the reasoning for it, but the majority are reluctant; there are a few that do, but this is rare at this moment in time and I hope they will change for the clients benefit as well as theirs in not losing further money for being so arrogant and naive and not thinking outside the box.

Nowadays lenders are not as ruthless as they were prior to 2008. There was a common rule of thumb within the sub-prime market that lenders would start repossession proceedings after a client missed 2/3 months payments, the charges and legal costs involved in these processes were added to the mortgage balance. Nowadays and with Government pressure, lenders have to prove to Judges they have tried to help householders in difficulty before a Judge will even look at repossession. (No Judge wants to put a family on the street, especially with having young children at school). More recently a lot of banks have introduced their own rescue schemes to help, which is very encouraging. Please also note that second/ third secured lenders usually have to get the agreement of the first lender to seek possession before instigating action. (So technically make sure you always pay your first lender).

I think it is fair to say that a third party working on behalf of the defendant can help with explaining your situation better to a Judge, as well as looking at your income and expenditure in more detail so as to offer a sensible offer. It's no good saying you can pay £x amount to pay off the arrears thinking this is what a Judge would like to hear. It has to be an affordable sensible offer, as this will be a Court

Order and if you fail to make the agreed payment, it does complicate matters at another hearing, strengthening the lenders position to ask for the repossession to go ahead.

At present, we offer a very unique repossession pack that we compile for the client to give to the Judge. We know what they're looking for regarding income and expenditure and detailed reasons explaining why the situation has happened, as well as our suggestion why the offer is sensible under the circumstances. Where we are different from solicitors and we have to point out again, we are not a legal team of experts but have extreme knowledge, is we charge a fee based on the house value. If the client has told us the truth, goes to Court and our offer is not accepted by the Judge we will refund the total fee paid so the client is not financially worse off, (is there a solicitor that would do this?) This is where we are different from the rest and some local solicitors have contracted us to do work on their behalf.

Claiming On Unenforceable Agreements

This seems to be the new topic in the claims industry. There are supposedly 1,000s of wrongly worded contracts as well as lack of information on agreements. Claims can be pursued against financial institutions such as loans, credit cards, car finance and supposedly mortgages. These Claims Management Companies will work on your behalf for compensation on particular areas such as mis-selling, unfair relationships, irresponsible lending, unfair charges and unenforceable agreements as well as payment protection insurance added without the client's knowledge as well as the blatant oversight of the banks under the Consumer Credit Act of 1974.

At the time of writing, I am an introducer to a certain company, but waiting for more evidence before I'm prepared to advise further. There have been many companies closed down by the Ministry of Justice for taking up front fees and not giving refunds or have gone out of business owing thousands to clients. Please be aware of the large fees some are charging. There are a few legal challenging issues taking place in the High/

Supreme Court and it will be interesting to see the outcome; however it is fair to say many individuals have claimed and been successful. Again, with the way we look at financial issues, sometimes a PPI claim can help resolve other financial issues for the client, for example:

A couple contacted us when Mr S found himself out of work as a builder and they were struggling to pay their unsecured Creditors. We have said previously that we do an in depth questionnaire and just by talking to them and finding out a little more about what they had done, we found they had paid a secured loan off the previous year. They had with them a final settlement and we found PPI had been included. As Mr S was Self Employed and Mrs S a Teacher at the time of taking the loan, they shouldn't have had this added. In short we claimed for mis-selling and received compensation which went towards paying of the major Creditors, leaving an acceptable surplus income to pay the others the normal monthly contributions on time, thus not destroying their credit history.

Individual Voluntary Arrangements (IVAs)

An IVA is a legally binding agreement via the court (but you don't have to go there) which is an alternative to bankruptcy where there is a good possibility Creditors will get a far better dividend than going bankruptcy. If you live in Scotland, they have what's called a Trust Deed (See after this section) but read the following, as technically they have the same rules as well as the benefits and what to be aware of. The principles are the same in trying to resolve your financial situation.

This is a legal secure way without your name going into the papers (in Scotland it does) to resolve your debt over a set number of years. This can range from 1 up to 5/6 years at present due to the economic climate as well as taking into account your age, job and if you own a house etc. Interest is frozen; your Creditors cannot pursue you for further monies (unless your circumstances change for the better) and you have a Supervisor who takes responsibility for running your arrangement throughout the term, working on behalf of you and the creditors.

Some of the drawbacks, in my opinion, to these arrangements are in these uncertain financial times as well as job insecurity they can be quite restrictive. A lot of people don't read the small print in the agreement they sign, that states usually that you agree not to miss more than 2/3 months payments not necessarily consecutively over the term of your IVA – or you could be made bankrupt.

Now there are quite a few good Supervisors in this country who have the overriding authority to help and agree to miss payments if there is a financial problem or health issue. It's in the Insolvency Companies interest to do so, due to the ongoing fees they receive and will lose if they don't resolve the situation. However there are a few who will stick to the rule and if you miss your contribution, your Creditors are informed and your credit file shows a failed IVA.

You could then be made bankrupt, destroying your credit file for a further 6 years. So let's say you've completed 3 years of a 5 year IVA and then you have financial problems and the Supervisor goes ahead with bankruptcy. Your file will show you have failed an IVA and then record a further 6 years that you have been made bankrupt. In total 9 years of poor history! I am not trying to put you off an IVA; they are very good but you have be aware of the consequences. Nobody can foresee 5 years into the future, but for instance, if you are in a high risk job where talks of redundancy or cut backs have been mentioned now, please beware.

If you have a property and there is equity, then on a 5 year IVA the norm on the fourth year is for you to agree to re-mortgage your house to the value of 85%. The problem at present (November 2010) is no lenders will do a remortgage until you are clear of your IVA by three years. Clients who are near the end of their agreements at present, are having to extend the term for a further year or so to pay back the equity they couldn't release.

What Debts can and cannot be included in an IVA?

All unsecured debts can be included in your IVA, this includes any County Court Judgments you may have or pending Charging Orders, Council tax arrears, Attachment of Earnings for most unsecured debts, income tax, PAYE, VAT etc. as long as it is personal debt. Please note if there is joint debt and only one does an IVA, the other party/partner becomes responsible for the debt remaining.

What you can't include is Child Support payments including any arrears, monies owed to the DWP (overpayments, housing benefit as well as Tax Credits etc), parking fines and many other related Magistrate Orders, like speeding convictions, fines for breach of the peace etc. Unfortunately one of the big debts that many of the younger generation have around their necks is Student Loans and these are not allowed either. (Unless taken prior to 1998)

Expenditure

With IVAs and depending on the Insolvency Company you use, you generally have quite an acceptable amount of income to live on, but very little for emergencies for the unexpected although far better than in a long term Debt Management Plan. The reason is the Creditors want you to succeed, but you need to work out exactly what you spend. Especially the little things that mount up that aren't standard on many forms, such as children's clubs and activities, special dietary needs, prescriptions/ herbal purchases, breakdown recovery; you may have gas boiler protection or insurance for electrical goods and house repairs etc. and these can add up to being quite considerable over the normal budget. (See income and Expenditure section). One item that's frowned upon and not allowed is for smoking; many Finance Companies say this is an area you don't need for basic living. Although I don't smoke; I have friends who have tried to stop and can't; all I'm doing is informing you of the standard practices within the industry.

Nominee

When you first apply for an IVA, the company looks at the prospect of it succeeding. Once this has been established, it's the job of the Nominee to collate all the information regarding income and expenditure, the reasons for the client's difficulty and to show an IVA has a better chance of succeeding where the Creditors will receive a larger dividend than a client going bankrupt. Once this has been arranged, a Creditors' meeting is set up to vote on the offer made. This is usually done by fax/internet and phone and you don't have to attend, but you need to be near a phone just in case a creditor might add a further restriction or not allowing for some expenditure. One common practice is to ask for 50% of any overtime or bonuses received and you might need to be aware and accept or reject this decision. If accepted then the role of the Nominee changes to what's called a Supervisor.

Interim Order

As I said at the beginning of the book, many don't seek help until the last minute. If there are pressures from

Creditors, like bailiffs or let's say a Charging Order is being applied for, you can apply for an Interim Order. (There is a fee to be paid). This means a Creditor can't go forward with his action until an IVA has been set up and put to the vote, although there is a time scale for this, these are usually organised by the Insolvency Company as they have to confirm they are processing the paperwork. Once again, don't leave it too late or you will regret it in future.

Creditors' Meeting

A meeting is held where the Creditors vote on whether to accept the offer. For the IVA to be approved, 75% of the votes have to say yes. Remember, it's not the number of Creditors; it's the level of debt. So if you have £100,000 debt, £75,000 votes have to say yes for it to proceed (See section on Dividends). The creditors that reject the IVA who are in the minority of 25% cannot pursue you further and have to accept the ruling and dividend.

Supervisor's Role

Technically the role of this person is to work primarily on behalf of you and the Creditors. In the main the Supervisors job entails watching over the IVA, making sure you pay on time, pay Creditors and be there for answer any questions or difficulties you may have during the period of the IVA. This person is authorised to help and decide on certain aspects or solutions that he thinks fit and report to Creditors if necessary.

So let's just say you have broken your arm and you don't receive full sick pay from your employer. Although you're not supposed to miss payments over the period of an IVA, a good Supervisor will understand your situation and will sanction a period of time to wait for you to return to work. This is the role of the Supervisor and he has the authority to do what's required for the benefit of you as well as the Creditors, so once again don't be frightened to talk to them; bear in mind that an annual report is sent to Creditors on how the IVA is progressing.

Dividend

When you have been told how much you have to pay on a monthly basis, the Creditors are offered what's called a dividend and this will be based on so many pence in the pound. In simple terms if you owe a £1 to your Creditor, but you can only afford to pay over the term of the IVA 30p, then the dividend offered is 30 pence in the pound.

Variation Order

In extreme cases, if you have started an IVA and it runs say two years and suddenly your employer has told you he needs to reduce your income, then understandably you're going to have difficulty maintaining your payments. In these circumstances the Supervisor, at his discretion, might go back to the Creditors and ask them to vary the agreement for reduced payments or extend the term. I have to say there are not many Insolvency Companies who like doing this as there is quite a lot of work involved, i.e. arranging the paperwork as well setting up another meeting for Creditors accept or fail the new offer. However let's say you were paying 60p in the pound (quite a good offer for an IVA) and you could only afford 30p then I would think there would be a good chance it would be accepted depending on the Creditor.

Look at Bankruptcy as well as IVA if you have rented property or no equity in your property

This is my opinion once again, but if you are in rented accommodation or have negative equity in your property and let's say you were looking at an IVA and told you had to pay £300 per month for 5 years, I would be seriously looking at going bankrupt for the following reasons:

As you read through this book and understand some of the implications, an IVA is usually for 5 years and you're not supposed to miss any contributions throughout the 60 month period. (And you know an IVA is an alternative to bankruptcy). If you went bankrupt, then the Official Receivers would ask/demand you pay approximately the same amount of disposable income (less £20) but you would only pay for 3 years! If during this time you have problems, like being off work, or have health issues or your partner has lost their job etc. then you can inform the Trustee appointed and reduce or stop making payments, but remember this agreement is only for 3 years, it can't be extended after this period.

Just to reiterate if you went Bankrupt in May 2010 paying £300 and in May 2011 lost your job and didn't find another one in the following two years, you would not have to pay further, as the 3 years would be up.

Trust Deeds (Scotland only)

A Trust Deed is for an individual living in Scotland. It has, in general, the same legal standing as an IVA in the UK although there are a few slight differences.

The legally binding agreement is usually for 3 years.

Although a Trustee more or less runs a Trust Deed, it has to be a Qualified Insolvency Practitioner who sets the process up.

Unfortunately the Trustee will advertise your intent in the Edinburgh Gazette where as in England this doesn't happen.

Finally whereas in England, Wales and Northern Ireland 75% of the Creditors have to agree to an IVA, with a Trust Deed the percentage is two thirds for acceptance.

Warning on DMP Agrrements
£42,000 of debt
You agree to pay £200 per month
This will take 254 months (min.) to pay off
21 years!!!!
Is it a good solution for you?

Debt Management Plans (DMP)

Although these plans are just a basic agreement between you and the Creditors, they can be a very good short term measure to help with your financial problems, but you shouldn't do a DMP for more than a few years (5 years) unless you have major equity in your house or have other property and land elsewhere. You should look at doing an IVA if your debts are over £10/15,000 (taking note of your job prospects etc. as we have mentioned above) but if this is the way you want to proceed, beware of how long you are going to be paying for. I have seen cases where they were going to last 30/40 years!

To give you a small example

If you had debts of £20,000 and paid £200 per month to a Debt Management Company, after deducting the monthly management fee, it would take you 121 months (10 years) to pay all your debt off and this is if management fees stay the same and interest has been frozen on all your accounts which is rare, bearing in mind even the charities have difficulties asking some Creditors to stop this scandal!!

The main problem I have with these plans is many individuals sign the agreement as a last resort and don't realise how long it's going to take to pay off their debts. Quite a few Debt Management Companies don't try hard enough to get the interest frozen or late payment charge stopped, so in some circumstances the debt increases and Creditors can still contact you direct, threatening further action if you don't improve your offer, sometimes asking for some of the monthly management fee you have been charged. This is usually a bluff to make you pay more and this is one of the reasons why many fail.

As I said earlier, Debt Management Companies live off your situation and there are two main fees charged. There is a set up fee which is usually the first 2 months surplus money available for Creditors (So Creditors don't receive any monies until the third payment has been received), and the other is an ongoing monthly management charge which on average within the industry is a minimum £35 or 17.5% of the contribution, whichever is the greater. So if you start paying £200 per month, the company takes £400 (first two months contributions) then deducts £35 thereafter, leaving £165 available to Creditors.

My personal feeling is Debt Management is a growing industry and there needs to be a reasonable standard charge for setting up a plan as well as a monthly fee for administering. Why do I say this? Although the fees on the above example are close to the maximum I would want a client to be charged.

The following shows what can be taken for higher contributions for doing the same amount of work:

Monthly payment	Set up charge	Monthly fee
£100	£200	£35
£300	£600	£53.50
£500	£1,000	£87.50
£750	£1,500	£131.25
£1,000	£2,000	£175
£1,500	£3,000	£262.50
£2,000	£4,000	£350

Just to reiterate the above regarding excessive fees, if you had 10 Creditors, the DM Company would have the same amount of negotiating to do whether the debts were £5,000 or £30,000.

But the difference over the year paying £200 and £1,000 a month are very significant as the following show:

Monthly Fee Contribution	First 2 months Fee	Monthly fee	Total in 1st year	Continuous after 1st year
£200	£400	£35	£820	£420
£1,000	£2,000	£175	£4,100	£2,100

As you can see there are significant fees when you're paying larger contributions and may I suggest you try to negotiate a better deal where more of your money is going towards paying your Creditors reducing the term left.

Going back to the aggressive threats from Creditors via phone, letters or worse solicitors saying they will not accept what's been offered can be distressing especially when you thought you were getting back on track with your finances. All I will say is tell them to contact your Debt management company as this is what you're paying them for and forward any correspondence you receive. If they are a decent company they will act and contact them and resolve the situation. Please check the debt management company you're going with to see if they are established as well as authorised, looking on the many blogs and scam sites on the internet for complaints against them. There will always be some disgruntled individual who's never happy or misunderstood what was said, but if you find too many negative comments, then I would advise you to go elsewhere.

In October 2010 the Office of Fair Trading put out a warning that they were looking into the practises of a 129 DM Companies. Although no specific details were mentioned, I do hope they will look at the fairness of contracts as well as fees and what some companies promise their clients.

Days before this book went to press, I had a client who was in a DMP and received a County Court Judgment from a certain Spanish Bank demanding more money than what he was paying. He contacted the DM Company about the summons and was told Creditors can do this. That was it, no more help, they didn't even offer to contact the lender to try to resolve the issue. I, however, went to Court with the client, explained he was on the bread line and he was offering as much as he could afford. The Judge agreed and the Court summons was thrown out. I also asked the Judge regarding the demand from the plaintiffs for £320 of costs and the Judge obliged with an emphatic refusal to allow them. So again, just because I defended my client in Court, we saved the fees from being added and stopped a lender's heavy handed approach.

It just shows to what lengths a Creditor will go to to pursue a debt, it also shows what a Debt Management Company should have done, didn't try or couldn't be bothered to do!

Can I be free of debt the minute the judge signs the paperwork?

Bankruptcy

Again this is my personal opinion. There is genuine fear of the word bankruptcy and many of the web sites you visit will portray the old fashion consensus that this should be the last resort and it is the most drastic decision you will ever make! And the terrible consequences! And all your possessions will all be taken! And you will have nothing left! Sorry for the next words: WHAT A LOAD OF BULL!!!!!!!! It doesn't help either that the majority of DM and IVA Companies advertise on the internet are also insinuating the same sort of fear, as they would rather make a living through the fees they charge over the years they have your custom. In all the 10 years I've been helping people go bankrupt, nobody has entered a client's home to take any possessions!! If there was the slightest possibility that this would happen, I would inform my client of what would be at risk e.g. a car/caravan etc.

It is also my belief that there should be two categories of bankruptcy. One for the simple fact that circumstances have taken their toll and there is no alternative for an individual but to go down this route. The other should be for the blatant and fraudulent individuals who use the system for their own advantage, ripping people off with the scams they pursue when they know they are defrauding vulnerable people. It is wrong to categorise bankruptcy as one type. All shouldn't be tarred with the same brush and feel you are being frowned upon and rejected. I ask all of my clients – have you tried your best to pay you're Creditors? And if, as is common, the answer is yes, I tell them to hold their head up high.

Bankruptcy to a lot of people over the age of 40 conjures up thoughts of failure and rejection from society, that it's your fault you got into this mess etc. These were the thoughts of many in the 70s and 80s when bankruptcy was very severe, embarrassing and a degrading prospect that stayed on your credit record for 15 years!

Bankruptcy can be the easiest way out of a financial and worrying nightmare that can finish as soon as the Judge has put pen to paper. But even if you do have property and little equity in the house, there is a very good chance you can keep your home. (See House Property & Equity)

Let's look at sub headings to get a perspective on the main issues people are concerned about:

Level of Debt to go Bankrupt

To go bankrupt you must have a minimum level of £5,000 unsecured debt. Although Judges don't like to make you Bankrupt for such a small amount, they may ask questions to justify the reason unless it's explained in the Statement of Affairs. In many cases it's because of threatening action from bailiffs who might have levied on goods or the threat of County Court Judgments or on very low benefits/ income and no opportunities to increase the household budget. As to a maximum level of debt, there isn't one, so it could be a million pounds or more.

The Courts and the Judges

This, for 99% of the individuals who are contemplating Bankruptcy, is by far the most frightening thought of all. The fear of going to Court and seeing a Judge sounds daunting, but we have to tell you it's not and it's very easy. Staff are very understanding and know what pressures you're under; some are a little automated in the way they do their job, but I think it's the norm if there is no variety within the work place. The first step in most Courts is for you to go to the General Office. In most cases you have to ring and make an appointment which could be weeks ahead, so beware. If we provide the service of completing your paperwork, we would coordinate everything and book your appointment. Your papers are checked by a Court Officer and if all is well, you sign a Statement of Truth and pay the required fee. Currently at the time of going to press this was £450 Official Receivers fee and £150 for the Court, (usually fees increase annually in April). You will then be directed to a waiting room to see a Judge.

First of all, don't worry, these Judges are usually what's called District Judges and you see them in a private room. They are not there to tell you off and quite frankly most who read your background leading up to your demise shake their heads and are dismayed at what lenders have done, in most cases putting you further into debt or not listening to you. (All for the sake of commission orientated sales). You're not going in front of a Judge with a wig, a red cape and a Jury looking over you. You will be seen by a man or a woman dressed the same as a normal solicitor. By the time you get to see them they would usually have looked at your Statement of Affairs and when you have sat down, will talk to you in an understanding and sympathetic manner and ask you if you know the consequences of Bankruptcy. Once you have said you do, they will look at the time and declare you Bankrupt that minute. (Last year we heard of a certain Judge who, on occasions, came around from his desk and opened the door telling the client it was a new start in life)

You will then be directed back to the office where you usually collect your certificate of Bankruptcy and might have a 5 minute telephone call with the Official Receivers. This is sometimes done straight away, or you might be called later at home, as they are usually in a different building or town and don't have the paperwork in front of them and they require certain information to contact the banks and financial institutions etc. They predominantly ask you three/four main questions. Do you have a house, a Bank account, a car, are you Self Employed. They will then agree a time to ring approximately two weeks later for a telephone interview lasting about 20 minutes. This is to resolve small issues when they might need further information on. Although if you have put on the events and circumstances, "Have no money can't afford to pay my debts", they will be asking for a lot more detail as they need a full background leading up to the day in Court.

If you are Self Employed and still run a business or have done so within the last 2 years, it is usual for you to be interviewed face to face as there will be a few more queries to answer with it being a business. There is a section within this book that explains in more detail the things you should be more aware of being Self Employed.

Due to the number of people going Bankrupt many Courts accept your paperwork in the morning, get you to sign a Statement of Truth and ask you to come back later the same day to collect your certificate of Bankruptcy. The Royal Courts of Justice in London do this as well as many busy Courts throughout the country and you don't have to see a Judge which relieves a lot of anxiety.

Northern Ireland process (This is the only difference)

When you want to go Bankrupt in Northern Ireland the only difference is the process. All the above remains the same: You have to take your Statement of Affairs to a Solicitor, sign a Statement of Truth, then you go to the Official Receivers where you pay the fee of £345 and gain a receipt; you then go to the County Court and show proof of payment and pay a Court fee of £115 and book a hearing which at the time of going to press was for the following Thursday. Again, you may or may not see a Judge, but you have to be present in the Court just in case he/she wants to ask you any questions. Also note while Bankrupt you must not leave the country without the permission of the Court.

Official Receivers Duty

The duty of the Official Receivers is to investigate the bankrupt's estate and ask some questions that need to be answered in more detail if the paperwork has not been completed fully. For the individual this is mainly done by having an approximate 20 minute phone call. It is the Official Receiver's job to contact the Creditors regarding your Bankruptcy. This can take many weeks, sometimes months and it's my opinion that as you have your certificate of Bankruptcy, you should photocopy it and when you receive any correspondence, attach a copy and send it back.

If you are getting extreme harassment from a Creditor and you have given your court reference number, inform the Receivers and they will contact them and the phone calls and letters should stop. Once these interviews have been completed it is the responsibility of the Official Receivers to inform the Creditors and inform them of any dividend, as well as sending a certificate of claim for the debt to be written off their accounts as a bad debt. If, however, there are funds available from the estate, then it's probable a Trustee will be appointed to complete the financial issues within a three year period.

Income Payments Order (IPO)
Income Payments Agreements (IPAs)

If you go Bankrupt and you have surplus money after normal living costs, you could be asked to make a contribution on a monthly basis for three years. (The agreement must be set up and started within the year of your bankruptcy) The good thing is that an IVA would take all your spare money to pay Creditors for 5 years. In Bankruptcy the Official Receiver/ Trustees would insist you pay approximately the same amount (less £20) of your spare income for 3 years, allowing you a small amount for ongoing living costs. Another good point I would like to make is – if you have a financial problem during your IPO/IPA and let's say you break your leg and can't go to work and don't receive full sick pay, or your hours are reduced etc, it is quite easy to change or stop your arrangement until you return to work. Trustees don't like this as this is where they make their money and try to put pressure on you to keep paying, *but* they can't override a genuine reason.

If you receive certain benefits such as Income Support, Pension Credits, Job Seekers Allowance, Working Tax Credit with a disability element you cannot be forced to pay anything. Some genuine people who want to pay something (especially the elderly) can if they wish offer a voluntary payment but this cannot be enforced if the bankrupt wanted to stop later.

Time in Bankruptcy

Usually most people who go Bankrupt do so for a maximum of one year, although if you are unemployed, on benefits, receiving Tax Credits it is possible you could be discharged earlier, sometimes within 6/8 months, though you can't ask for this to happen as it's up the Official Receiver.

In general, if you have young children and are looking after them full time, then it is unlikely within the year your income will increase; the same goes with someone who is disabled or retired on basic pensions – what would be the point of keeping them bankrupt.

Self Employment in Bankruptcy

Although this can be a complicated issue, let's just put the basics forward in short. There are many who think they can't continue to be Self Employed after they go or are made bankrupt.

This is wrong; you can and there are many taxi drivers as well as individuals in the building trade who have done so and still trade. The main reasons for not allowing you to continue is if your present and previous accounts leading to your Bankruptcy are not up to date. The Official Receivers take a dim view of this and work on the principle that a person running a business should be accountable and have knowledge of their financial situation. Make sure these are completed to show at a meeting.

In my opinion have an independent Bookkeeper/ Accountant complete them as it helps with the enquiry as usually the O/R asks their professional opinion if there is any reason why you shouldn't still trade. Another mis-conception is you can't have a bank account- wrong! You can, although limited. There are many reasons why you're allowed to keep trading and here are a few ideas:

Let's say you were a promotional business with printing machines, computers, as well as a vehicle to deliver your product. If you had to go Bankrupt because you were owed a large amount of money from a client and they ceased trading, then the reasons for being insolvent are common and not your fault.

You may have been a contractor working for a building firm who has gone out of business; these factors can't be foreseen all of the time. In this situation you could stay Self Employed and keep all your equipment as these are the tools of your trade. It is up to the Official Receivers to agree or demand that you stop trading. If you continue to be Self Employed however, you must show on letter heads and advertisements your name within the trading business e.g. John Example trading as 12345 builders.

You will be told to stop trading if you have blatantly spent money taking advantage of an overdraft or taken credit facilities without earning income, or show the reason for the business failure. This could be due to a contract that hasn't materialised or, as is common nowadays, the bank has changed its lending criteria and refused the promised funds.

Having Bank Accounts

There is an issue here that although you should get a Bank account after you're made Bankrupt, in my opinion, it's much harder after the event, as the Bank will do a credit check and see your financial situation and usually refuse you. At the time of printing this book, Barclays would allow you to open an account and keep it after you go Bankrupt. We have however found when they have gone Bankrupt, in some areas, they've been refused. At present there are only two main Banks who allow you to have a proper basic account and these are the CO-OP and Barclays. They are basic, but you can do Standing Orders and Direct Debits etc. And on-line banking (Please note if you owe them money you cannot Bank with them). There are a few Building Societies you can apply to but they take ages to clear funds before having access to your money. Some people who have problems ask a relative if they can use one of their accounts, but this is going to stop in the near future due to the tightening restrictions on money laundering. Although you may have problems getting an account, another short term measure would be a Pre-Payment card. You can then have your income paid directly and use for every day expenses, but be aware they are very expensive. Once again, look at your future as to how you would use this type of facility.

Bank Accounts within the Bankruptcy

When you go Bankrupt and the Official Receivers have been informed, there is a form of a Chinese whisper that goes round all the Banks/Financial Institutions informing them of your demise and asking for information on any accounts you have or had in the past two years as well as balances held, including ISA's, Personal Pension, Endowment Plans, Savings Accounts in your name as well as in joint.

Unless there are significant amounts of monies, usually more than what's required for normal living expenses, the Official Receivers are not interested. It's a misconception that it's the Official Receivers who freeze the average account. It is the banks that stop them as they all have different rules regarding a bankrupt.

If you go bankrupt, don't leave very much in the account as it can take many days to access your money. None of the banks will rarely give you access until they have been informed by the Official Receivers that they have no interest. This means the Official Receivers have to send a fax to the bank authorising the funds to be released, it's then up to the bank to decide if they will allow them to continue to have an account and unfortunately the majority don't at present. I have known banks to send a letter enclosing a cheque for the balance informing the client they don't want them as a customer, even when they don't owe the particular bank any money or have any loan or overdraft facility.

What I find strange is banks make money from others having balances. If there are no overdraft facilities (and there shouldn't be due to the restrictions on bankrupts), why are there very few allowing accounts in this day and age when it's safe to do so? We all know there are facilities without cheques and if you have an account with a debit card with no overdraft and you use it and there are no cleared funds, the purchase or withdrawal is refused. So why are they so unhelpful? Another factor is the vast majority of bankrupts never want credit ever again and want to stay in the black.

If you own a Car

In bankruptcy you are allowed a car up to the value of approximately £1,500 – £2,000 based on auction price, so you can get to work and back – this is the average/norm. However, if you had to supply your own car for your job and it's in your contract of employment and you are expected to travel around the country like a rep, then you need to discuss with the examiner your need for a more reliable vehicle due to the miles you have to do; they are fair and have discretion in this situation as if you lose your vehicle then you could lose your job. You will probably have to make your appeal convincing and might have to show your employment contract as well as a letter from your employer.

If, however, you have a car and its worth say £10,000 the Official Receivers will allow you approximately £2,000 to buy a car and yours would be sold at auction to release monies.

When Self Employed, the above criteria are totally different regarding the term tools of your trade (your vehicle) as you can keep it for your business. We helped a certain Self Employed Taxi Driver /Chauffer who was a sub-contractor and under the terms of receiving work he had to have a Mercedes no more than 5 years old. He was allowed to keep it as it was his business and was valued at £25,000.

Having a Car on HP, Contract Hire or PCP Contracts etc

In the past, most Finances Companies with secured loans on a vehicle used to allow you to keep your car, as long as you didn't have any history of missed payments prior to bankruptcy. If you miss your commitments, most would take action to recover the vehicle as soon as possible as they couldn't claim for any outstanding monies owed in the future.

Unfortunately times have changed; most allow you to keep your car but you must contact your Finance Company and speak to the insolvency department. You need to ask what is their criteria regarding individuals going bankrupt. If they tell you they will allow you to keep your car under certain conditions, demand confirmation in writing – if not, get the person's name and email/fax number and send them notification confirming the conversation you had with that person. Emails are now the best way as these can be traced, whereas letters can go missing or Creditors could say they never received any correspondence. Unfortunately, last year, a client did as I asked and three months after the Finance Company demanded the car back; she had no proof of the conversation. We had a very hard time fighting for the client to keep the car so beware, if you need it for work and then find yourself without one, this could be embarrassing as well as possibly losing your job.

Cars financed on DLA

This sounds crazy, but if you have a car on DLA, it's been given to you to help with your disability in getting from A to B. Can you believe the following? You can only keep your car if you are on high rate disability. If you are on the lower rates, you will unfortunately have your vehicle taken off you. I know this sounds stupid but for some reason this is the rule. So, if you are registered disabled and thinking of going bankrupt, please check with your provider before proceeding so you can make alternative arrangements if this happens.

Bankruptcy Restriction Order (BRO)

BRO's are very serious. It means that the restrictions put upon you in bankruptcy will be extended for a period of years after the standard one year. If you were thinking of being a Director after bankruptcy has finished, this will not be allowed until your restriction has been lifted.

This was in the past rare, although now is becoming more common; usually it's when you have deliberately used money or gained finance knowing you couldn't afford to pay it back. It is the same if you've been Self Employed or run a business, knowing you were over trading or couldn't show evidence you were getting further work.

The other issue the Official Receivers frown upon or class as severe is for the Self Employed not having your accounts up to date. Get them done before you go Bankrupt! If a BRO is discussed then to save further costs, you will be asked to accept a voluntary period of time (This could be 1 to 15 years). If you refuse, you will be forced to go in front of a Judge to defend your case. We have to say from experience, try to negotiate a lower time frame as it is very rare you will win in Court. The worst restriction order we have come across has been 9 years and this was a blatant misuse of Inland Revenue funds.

For individuals BROs are unusual but, if you have deliberately spent money or taken credit knowing you cannot afford to pay it back, you will be asked to explain this situation. If you kept spending on your credit cards and catalogues up to the time of going Bankrupt then it could be seen you were feathering your own nest so to speak.

Example

To give you a better idea, let's say you bought a three piece suite on interest free credit a week before you went bankrupt, this would understandably be seen as taking a liberty before the bankruptcy. Believe it or not, without our knowledge, some clients have used available credit such as maxing out their credit card or overdraft to pay the Court fees. One of the first questions many Official Receivers ask is how you paid your fees for Bankruptcy and will ask to see previous Bank and credit card statements. If they find you had done the above they would view this as very serious.

On Benefits

When you are on benefits it is very hard for the individual to find the money to go bankrupt. It is ironic that when you have debt and no job, you have to pay. At the time of publishing this book the 2 fees totalled £600. (You can't do a joint Bankruptcy). Invariably, if you are on Job Seekers Allowance or Child /Tax Credits/Income Support you may only have to pay £450. **We must stress, however, the Court Officer needs to see proof in writing confirming you are on benefits and the letter has to be dated less than a month before your court date.** The reason for this is the system has been abused. In the past if you were on Family Tax Credits your award was for the whole year or if you were on Job Seekers Allowance you had a card as proof. Some have submitted paperwork to save £150 Court fee. **You will also need to take 3/6 months Bank statements showing the payments made into your bank account.** If, however, you have assets less than £300 you should look at applying for a Debt Relief Order. Please see this section.

The Consequences and limitations of bankruptcy

Although there are a few limitations in going bankrupt the main areas to look at are:

- You're not allowed to borrow more than £500 without telling the person/bank you are a Bankrupt.

- You're not allowed to be an MP

- A School Governor

- In some vocations you may not be allowed to manage a Company

- Or be a Director of a Company while in Bankruptcy.

You can, however, resume a Directorship once discharged as long as you don't have a BRO.

House Property & Equity: (Extremely Important!)

If you have been made or have gone bankrupt, or thinking of doing so and you own a house, there are a few issues that have to be looked at. If there is no equity in the property and you are paying your Mortgage/Secured loans, then the good news is you will most likely be able to keep your home as your debts in bankruptcy are for unsecured. If, however, you have equity in your property we have to look at a few scenarios based on the following. **Once again, think about your future goals, not just the problem at hand.**

PLEASE, PLEASE BE AWARE, if you think 'O' my partner has a Mortgage on the property and it's in their sole name and I'll just go Bankrupt as I don't own any property. Beware!! If you've lived together for more than 3 years, the Official Receivers will proportionalise some or half of the equity as yours, especially if both of you earn the same income, or you earn more than your partner, as they will argue that you have paid towards the upkeep and helped increase the value of the property over time due to your financial input. No ifs or it won't happen – IT WILL!!!!

We had a client who wanted to go Bankrupt; his wife inherited the family home when her parents passed away. She hadn't worked for thirteen years but he had paid for new windows as well as guttering. When we told him about the equity, he didn't believe this was right and so we told him to contact the Official Receivers Office who confirmed what would happen.

The Official Receivers who deal with your financial estate have a duty to recover monies for the Creditors; they will ask you to get two valuations on your property and would usually get an independent one themselves, or might look on line at the many web sites that show the history of what has sold recently in your street. The average of the three would then determine the amount the property is valued at. Please contact us regarding how to ask for a valuation to save fees that many estate agents may charge.

WARNING! Very important!

If you know someone who has gone bankrupt prior to 2011 and they had equity in their house and kept the property, please beware of new changes/rules from January 2011 regarding equity issues. You must take advice as there are serious consequences if you don't know all the different areas that have changed. Many debt advisory web sites will take a while to make the changes necessary so be careful. If you want to contact us we will advice on your particular circumstances.

Previously, although in the following examples we show that in some cases there are just a few thousand pounds of available equity after contingency fees etc. The Official Receivers can now apply to the court for a Charging Order for the whole amount which will stay on the property until the house is sold or remortgaged, they will also claim statutory interest on the amount until repaid. It will be up to the Official Receiver/Trustee to decide to go down this root. What I have been informed of, is that if there is equity, then the Official Receivers may withhold their decision deciding on the valuation of the property in 2 years and 3 months, this would allow in many cases an increase in property prices over the time frame to demand a larger increase of equity to be secured against. Again as this is a new change/rule that has just come in as this book was going to print, the vague answers to a definite confirmation as to what or if they would take this action, are not explicit enough. My first thoughts on this matter are: that if an offer from a third party was made, the Official Receivers/Trustees should be working on behalf of the creditors and if an offer in today's economic climate was made for the majority required, this should be accepted, as not doing so, would prolong the waiting time to pay a dividend to creditors if a Charging Order was enforced, which could stay on for many years before monies were released. From my sources it looks as if the final decision rests wholly with each individual Receiver. This worries me as experience in the past shows some Receivers don't work by the same set of rules. It could be (and these are my thoughts thinking out a loud so to speak) but he could look at the area in which the property is situated, working on the basis of house prices increasing better in some areas than others. Another disappointment / irritation which I mention under the sub title of "Trustees", is that once a Charging Order has been granted, a Trustee will be appointed and take a fee for watching over the order until finalised (more fees for doing very little) Again this is my opinion.

Example:

Let's say the quotes are £110,000, £125,000 and £130,000 then the average price of the house is £121,666 (add up the three valuations and then divide them by three). If the property has a £100,000 Mortgage, this means there is equity of £21,666. You then have to add any penalties, for instance, you might have a fixed rate, discounted or tracker Mortgage with penalties as well as any early redemption charges. For this example we will say for easy maths that these are £1,666 meaning we have £20,000 left as equity.

I need you to bear in mind the following in this example: To force a sale by the Official Receiver or Trustee will incur significant fees; these will be recovered out of the bankrupt's share of the estate, once sold, before any Creditors get a dividend. (But, with the new rule they might not pursue this course of action). The costs incurred will be for professional fees in the extra work involved such as a house valuation, legal fees, Court hearing, bailiffs, and Estate Agents for selling the property as well as locksmiths and legal costs on completion. On average these will be at least £4,500/£5,000 on a £130,000 valued house, higher if the property is more expensive, as the majority of Estate Agents take a fee based on the price of the house sold. At going to press Estate Agents were charging on average 1.25%, so a property worth £250,000 the fee for this alone would be £3,125!!

Here are a few situations you may have to consider if you go Bankrupt, based on the above example:

In One Person's Name

If the house is in your name only, then the Official Receivers will ask you to see if a family member or friend/

third party is prepared to buy the interest in the property. In the above example the Official Receiver/Trustee would probably be looking for an offer of £15,000 as the costs of not accepting would incur the extra £5,000 to pursue. Although as we have warned above, the Official Receivers might, instead of accepting, put a Charging Order for £20,000 on the property to gain the full amount when the house is sold or refinanced. But at what cost to the creditors?

In Joint Names and both going Bankrupt

If the house was in joint names, but both were on the Mortgage, then the above criteria would still apply in finding the same amount of money i.e. £15,000, or the Official Receivers / Trustee might go down the root of a Charging Order as above.

Joint Names and only One Going Bankrupt: (Married Couple Mr going Bankrupt)

If the house was in joint names and Mr went bankrupt, then you have to look at this situation in more detail. Mrs Share in the property cannot be used or touched so in the example we have £20,000 equity. This means Mrs £10,000 is technically safe as the non bankrupt's share. If Mrs cannot raise the £7,500 to buy the equity (£20,000 less £5,000 equates to £15,000 divided by two), then a Court hearing could be instigated to force the property up for sale, but Mrs would technically have an interest/say in the house sale as a lower offer would reduce the non Bankrupt share of the equity.

There was a rule of thumb (but again this may change shortly) as to how long you have to resolve equity issues. If there are no children in education living in the household then the Official Receivers/Trustees could be looking at resolving equity within a 12 month period. If, however, there are children living in the house up to school or university age, then they would be looking to resolving the issue within 2 years and 3 months, the same that has been suggested with the new rules. By law, a Bankrupt's financial estate has to be completed within 3 years from the start of Bankruptcy. So if you couldn't find the funds over the period allowed, the Receivers/Trustees would have to apply for a Charging Order before the 3 year limit.

Property with Negative Equity
This is a very difficult dilemma and can be one of the hardest questions/decision you have to decide on for your future.

As I keep repeating myself yet again, you have to look at the future and this is one of the biggest areas/decisions you have to make. You have to look at your job security, your children's schooling, is it close to the next school, college or university? Has it a good reputation? Are you close to your relatives? Are your neighbours great etc? These are major questions and the consequences you will have to live with far into the future and well after you're discharged.

Finally, another **BIG and one of the most difficult questions** of all, and sorry to mention this when you could be already stressed and looking for options and answers and I'm not a marriage guidance counsellor (although sometimes I have had to be the arbitrator), but this is for your own individual benefit for the future.

And the BIG question

Is your relationship with your partner **very** secure? I'm not talking about just being in love, it has to be more than that, as there will be friction if things don't pan out the way you thought and the consequences are extremely severe if you separate and the property has to be addressed later, well after discharge and the following will explain the dilemma.

Again, we have to put forward two scenarios to help you understand the implications of what I have asked.

Example:

Let's say you have a house worth £150,000. You have a Mortgage of £140,000 a Secured loan £30,000 in total £170,000 Secured Debt, leaving you in negative equity of £20,000.

The good news is you can keep the property as long as you keep paying your secured repayments on time.

Now we have to look at your future. When you have the above situation, you have to remember that if you decide to keep the house you are going to be in negative equity well after the one year of Bankruptcy. You will also have to remember that if you want to move in the future, then you're going to have to wait for the value of your home to go up substantially in order to settle the Secured loans, or the lender might not allow the sale to complete and you will also have to gain a future deposit on the next property.

So let's say the average house price will increase at 3% per annum. This means to settle just the outstanding loans will take you over 5 years! If you're hoping to move and buy another like for like property and let's say the next house is valued at £200,000 (based on the same house increase over the same period), you will need a deposit of £40,000! (80% loan to value as you won't get a 95% Mortgage). This now means you will have to stay and live in the house for 9 years to gain the sum required to move (£200,580) and this does not include stamp duty, moving costs, Estate Agents or legal fees!

Now, if you're happy where you live, your neighbours are great, the school is OK, travelling costs are reasonable, then you have to commit to this length of time. If you don't think this is possible, then you might want to look at moving into private rented property. I say this because at least you can choose where you live and you're not offered somewhere undesirable by the Council or Housing Association where you might not have a choice. You might find renting could be far less than the monthly outlay of the secured loans.

If this option is taken, then you could hand the keys back to the lender (before or within a few months of going bankrupt) and have the negative equity (as it won't be secured once the keys are handed back) added to your Bankruptcy, thus giving you a fresh start for the future with no financial worries or negative equity liabilities.

Remember, if you give up your house or can't afford to pay the loans and have it repossessed after your Bankruptcy has finished, then the lender can pursue you for the outstanding balance once the property has been sold. You will have no say in the sale of the property, so the existing negative equity, repossession costs as well as a lender possibly selling the house far less than what it's worth could amount to many thousands more than you expected it to sell for. Again, a very important decision has to be made, not just at the time of Bankruptcy, but for the future of your immediate family living with you.

In the event you want to add the negative equity into your Bankruptcy, there are areas that need to be addressed before hand and I would suggest you take advice on this matter from specialists like us. Solicitors are not the people to go to unless they are experienced in insolvency (and there aren't many). We have certain proven ideas as to planning a move to another house and could save some embarrassment regarding your credit file, Letting Agency and future landlord.

Let's look at a more significant and major negative equity problem. Let's say you have a house worth £200,000. You have a Mortgage of £160,000, a Secured loan of £80,000, another one for £25,000 and let's just say a Creditor has placed a Charging Order on your house for £10,000.

In total the Secured loans on the property are £275,000! (Please don't think this is unusual as this is nothing compared to what I have experienced by banks adding security for business overdrafts, loans, Charging Orders or Personal Guarantees etc), meaning you could have negative equity of £125,000!

In this situation you have a big problem and based on the same 3% increase per annum and let's be fair this is a very generous increase in house prices, you have to stay in the property for over 9 years to gain enough to pay just the secured debt! If you wanted to move to another house in the future (like for like again) valued at say £320,000, then you will need to have a deposit of 20% totalling £64,000 based on a 80% LTV Mortgage which will be the maximum at present in today's economic times. So to do this you would need to stay in the property for an additional 6 years! In total 15 years before moving!

This doesn't include Stamp Duty, moving costs or legal fees! It is your choice, and once again you have to make a very hard decision for the long term future regarding the massive negative equity you have in this scenario.

Just to add another dimension to the above, the creditor with a Charging Order on the house for £10,000 could, although very unlikely, apply for what's called a Forced Sale. This means that you could lose the house in this event, although a Judge would have to approve this, but just think if the charge was £50,000?

And sorry to add to the burden of the dilemma above, but if the Official Receivers thought the Bankrupt had a good income and realised you were paying say three quarters of it on Mortgage and Secured loans, he might put pressure on you to give the property up, as rented accommodation could be significantly cheaper than the payments and this would instigate an Income Payments Order where Creditors might receive a dividend. This is more likely to happen if you are single or living in a large house or exclusive area.

Repossession Liabilities:

As I have just mentioned, the consequences regarding negative equity and giving your keys back to the lender can have catastrophic problems in the future if not done right. I would like to emphasise what happened to a couple who kept their property.

A couple had £20,000 of negative equity when the housing market was at its highest; (130% mortgage) They both went bankrupt and I suggested they gave the property up and add the negative equity as I thought the house was already overvalued. Their reason for keeping the house was in a few years the property would increase as well as they were going to inherit monies from Mrs side of the family when her mother passed away. Two years later the mother died but she bequeathed her whole estate to her only son as the above couple had borrowed money from her a long time ago and this was through an equity release plan where the lender had a percentage of the property once sold. They have now divorced, given the house back and the lender who sold the property accepted £100,000 less than what the mortgage was. They are now both being chased for £112,000 and will probably have to go bankrupt again.

Removing the Official Receivers Interest in the Property

If you stay in your property and have come to an arrangement to buy the interest, the Official Receivers at the beginning of your Bankruptcy would have put an interest/caution on the Land Registry so that you wouldn't be able to sell it without their knowledge. To get this removed, you have to pay the agreed amount or a nominal fee of £1 (even if in negative equity) and pay the legal costs for both parties, the Official Receivers, as well as your own Solicitors (approximately £700 depending where you live). Please note it is advisable, if this arrangement has been concluded, that you pay the fee straight away, as if your property went up in value over the three years there could be an increase in equity, thus gaining possible further monies.

Trustees:

A Trustee is usually appointed when there is an Income Payments Order made, or equity in property or other valuables like insurance policies, vehicles, land, expensive paintings etc. At present the Official Receivers don't have the resources to watch over these matters.

As far as I am concerned this is an area that should be changed and kept within the Official Receivers remit as I personally disagree in giving carte blanche fees to Trustees who are appointed. If there is an easier way to make money out of the unfortunate bankrupt as well as the Creditor suffering further loss of dividend, this is it. It is very rare, for instance, if an Income Payments Order was made that any Creditor will receive a significant dividend if an individual was only paying £100 per month. In total, over the three year period, there would be £3,600 collected and the Trustee would receive well over half of this amount in fees. Is it right that this should happen? Is it me, or is someone enjoying the bureaucratic system we have in every area of Government and Crown affairs, where fees are for the boys instead of paying the unfortunate Creditors more.

Where I think it should be more rewarding for Creditors is having a vote on what the fees should be, like an IVA. Trustees are like old fashioned accountants who work on the basis of turnover/debt. So if one goes bankrupt for say £140,000 and has 6 Creditors, there would be a administration charge of at least £20,000. Now let's say a bankrupt has £30,000 of debt and has 15 Creditors then the work involved on the administration side would only be approximately £5,000. So the Trustee in the above two scenarios makes more on the larger debt, but has less work to do sorting out the estate. Again another sore point as there's something wrong here.

Renting Property

If you're in accommodation owned by the Council or Housing Association, you will probably be able to stay in the property as long as there were no arrears, or had come to an arrangement with them.

If you are in private rented property I would advise you to look at your tenancy agreement to see if there is any clause if you were declared bankrupt. May I suggest you talk to the landlord as he could be informed by the Official Receivers to ask if there are any monies owed, as they would/ should be included in the Statement of Affairs as they would not be able demand them in the future. It has been our experience that few who are receiving rent on time and see the property looked after will have any problems allowing you to stay, and understand and appreciate your honesty as well as your dilemma in talking to them.

You're Job and your Employer

It is not a duty on your part to tell your employer that you have gone Bankrupt; the Official Receivers in our experience, very rarely do this either. As far as we are concerned, that's the end of it.

Although there is an issue that may cause concern regarding the tax you pay when you are Bankrupt, within the first 6/8 months of the financial tax year. The Official Receivers claim the tax you had deducted from your gross pay and inform the Inland Revenue of his request for this amount. The Tax Office then has to notify your employer of your new tax coding and the tax is paid directly into your Nett pay (don't think you've got a bonus, you haven't). You then have to pay this amount to the Official Receivers/Trustee every month until the end of the following tax year. Your code then returns to normal and off takes resume. This is where there could be questions by small business owners or wage departments, as they might ask the Inland Revenue, as well as you, why this unusual occurrence has happened. Under data protection, technically they shouldn't discuss personal details, but it is open to the general public as your name appears in the London Gazette.

Don't ask me why this is done; as far as I am concerned, this is another bit of bureaucracy gone mad. This means the Official Receivers have to notify the Inland Revenue of the claim for tax deducted, the Revenue has to change the tax code and notify the employer at the beginning, as well as after, when it reverts back to normal and there is labour on the part of your employer to do both alterations!

Why the Inland Revenue, who receive it from the employer, can't pay this sum directly to the Official Receivers/ Trustee is beyond me! Talk about the Government wanting to save money this would save millions in time and money when you think there is a person going Bankrupt every 4 minutes in this country at the time of printing this book. It must take an employee of the Inland Revenue more than half an hour's work for each case to expedite this action alone, and this doesn't include the employer's labour costs, especially for the small business who will want to ask many time consuming questions to make sure the instruction is correct as they would be worried about being liable after the event.

Name in Paper (not in local paper)

This is another area that worries a lot of people. All I can say is it has to go in the newspaper by law and apart from Police and Prison Officers and other high ranking jobs for security reasons, they are the only ones who don't get advertised. In the olden days a black box would surround your name to make it stand out on the page. Nowadays your name is in normal print and it only goes in the London Gazette NOT IN YOU LOCAL PAPER!! The reason it's advertised is Bankruptcy was originally set up for the Self Employed. In the olden days your name was printed so anyone who was owed money had to inform the Receivers.

Nowadays it is mainly the general public who are going Bankrupt and they know the debts they owe or can do a credit check on themselves. This is still the advice on the internet of the old days and still hasn't changed to date, once again putting concerns on the individual.

Problems after 6 years
Could be asked to admit Bankruptcy on a job or loan application

Job Application

I have great reservations whether this is legal. In my opinion and I am not going to ask you to deceive or lie and again I am not a Solicitor or have any legal certificates, but as bankruptcy is **not a Criminal Offence**, I feel asking this question on or in an interview for a job could be a legally challenging issue on a point of employment law as it could be classed as discriminating. Again, there are many simple minded folk who still think bankruptcy is criminal and they need to grow up and live in the real world as this needs to be dispelled.

Just to emphasise a point, I have helped bank cashiers go bankrupt and they keep their jobs and they still touch money, help and advise customers and are not questioned about their personal finances or private lives. I would also add that when you apply for a job (other than in the financial sectors), where do you sign an authority for a potential employer to allow them to do a credit check on you? So why ask the question?

Loan Application

Again, when applying for a loan or a Mortgage, why should a lender be able to ask if you have ever been made Bankrupt? They all do credit checks and see the past 6 year's history. So why remind people of past experience where many would like to forget, especially if widowed, had severe health problems like cancer, divorced or had difficulties with employment causing the bankruptcy originally. Why should they be persecuted forever?

Although it might be a small percentage of applicants, this could be an area in these economic times where a bank is refusing a loan.

Bankruptcy is not a Criminal Offence!

I am repeating myself here; Bankruptcy is not a Criminal Offence!!! You can emigrate to Australia, New Zealand, Canada the USA as well as many other countries and many clients have done so and yes, you can go on holiday!

Although remember, if you live in Northern Ireland you need permission while Bankrupt.

Going Bankrupt = Debt goes away:

When you go bankrupt all your unsecured debts are not your responsibility anymore. It's the Official Receiver's duty to contact the Creditors on the Statement of Affairs. No Creditor can demand money, ring you up, send you letters or send debt collectors or bailiffs to your door. It is against the law!! We would, however, remind you to divulge all your debts or there can be serious consequences if found later.

Bankruptcy In Scotland

Again, in general, bankruptcy is more or less the same as in England, Northern Ireland and Wales once you have gone through the process; the only differences are as follows:

The minimum level of debt you must have to go bankrupt is £1,500

The fee for going Bankrupt is £100

You have to have an order of payment through the Courts (like a CCJ in England, Northern Ireland and Wales) it must be an expired charge which follows a Court decree for an outstanding amount or a Poinding like a summary (warrant) for Council Tax arrears. (In plain English, if you have an order to pay via a Court Order and you don't conform, you can go Bankrupt)

Instead of the Official Receivers administering your bankruptcy in England, Northern Ireland and Wales there is what's called the Accountant in Bankruptcy who is a Court Official that administers the work.

If you don't have the above criteria in place, you can't go Bankrupt.

Bankruptcy Living Abroad

A lot of people don't realise that if you emigrate and hope to pay your Creditors from afar, but for some reason your finances change for the worst, you can go Bankrupt without coming back to the UK.

The main stipulation is that you must do this within three years of leaving and there is an expense that has to be borne and this is for your paperwork to be signed by a legal person in the country you are living in and you also need to have someone in the UK to be your Power of Attorney.

This is a very specialised area and we have to say we think we are the only ones who have the vast experience of doing this, although expensive, you would have to weigh up the cost of flights back to the UK, accommodation as well as your return journey against the reasonable fees for completing the paperwork on your behalf and placing your petition with the Royal Courts of Justice. Any other questions you may have – contact us. Once again, a further book on this subject will be published soon.

Debt Relief Order (DRO)

Debt Relief Orders are for people who have very little money or minimalistic assets. This is more for the very low paid worker or person on long term benefits but it's just like bankruptcy.

To be suitable for a DRO you have to have less than £15,000 of unsecured debt, not be a homeowner, have less than £300 worth of assets apart from a car that can be worth up to £1,000 (at auction price) and have less than £50 per month surplus income after very basic living costs. Finally you must have at least one Count Court Judgment against you to qualify

What does it cost?

Sorry to say this, but this is for the very vulnerable low paid, the fees for a DRO are £90 and paid direct to the Official Receivers and you don't have to visit the Court and there are no further fees to pay for like normal Bankruptcy.

Who administers a DRO?

The Official Receivers deal direct with you and contact the Creditors on your behalf. As the paperwork is quite basic to complete, it can only be done by the free approved charities – these are the CCCS, CAB or Pay Plan. This is only right as the fees companies would have to charge for completing the paperwork would be far greater than the £90 fee.

Full & Final Settlements

If you have, or can get, a lump sum through friends or family and you could raise approximately 30/50% of your total outstanding debt, there is a possibility you might be able to negotiate a settlement with some of the Creditors whereby the Lender accepts a one off payment for the debt. (This varies depending on the Creditor, age and level of debt)

In the past when we negotiated on these cases we demanded that part of the agreement was the client's credit file would show it was completely settled. Nowadays, although you should still ask, most Creditors will accept a payment but note on your credit file that it's a partial settlement. This will show the remaining balance on your file but they will not demand any further monies in the future.

In my opinion if you have many Creditors, it would be best to have a third party negotiate on your behalf as the experience of talking tough and offering them a carrot to accept in a limited time frame, or it's withdrawn, does have its rewards. To negotiate hard and to get the best deal, have the money available to pay within 48 hours of acceptance and we do specialise in this area.

The older the debt the better chances of a larger reduction being accepted. In May of 2010, I negotiated for a client a two year old debt with a credit card balance of £10,200, the Creditor accepted just over £2,100 as a partial settlement. It can be done, although the outstanding debt will show on his credit file for another 4 years, he won't be harassed any further.

Self Employed

There are a few more issues to look at regarding debt as a proprietor business as well as a Director of a company. In the main course of business we all have good Accountants to keep our personal tax liabilities to a minimum. However the problem is when you want to use one of the many solutions above you have to prove you can afford to pay your Creditors. Suddenly applying for an IVA is going to be difficult as the Inland Revenue have to be informed; suddenly you declare a substantial increase in your income which might alert the Revenue to ask a few questions.

A further book will be published in the near future to go into more depth about being Self Employed or a limited company, as well as many suggestions on how to run a business/company and the pit falls to look out for; I will go into more detailed about debt issues, owing money as well as customers paying late. Until then, if you have any worries or concerns, please have no hesitation to contact us and we will help answer and advise on your predicament.

Pre Payment Cards

These types of cards were introduced to help students on gap years as well as holidaymakers who had limited banking facilities. Like having an electron card, that's not welcome in many places in this country as well as abroad, or having no bank account what so ever. You can pre-load your card by paying cash at a bank and family can pay money in if there was an emergency, but it has the benefit of being a Visa or MasterCard, so it's accepted around the World just like a credit card.

These are becoming more popular now, but are expensive regarding the fees charged, when you think it's your own money you are using. On the plus side, you're independent and this could be classed as a short term measure. The good news with some cards is that you can have your wages paid directly into the account for easy access, but many won't do Standing Orders or Direct Debits. However you can use them to pay for everyday items like supermarket shopping, phone payments, as well as buying goods on the internet.

Note: Please look at the various cards on offer by using the many comparison web sites and think about how often you are going to use the card as fees can be charged every time you use it.

Example

If you draw out say £10 every other day, they will charge a percentage or a flat fee of approximately £1 per withdraw, thus charging you £3/4 per week to get your own money out; others charge a monthly subscription, others do both. So be very careful and research.

More Examples Of Solutions To Problems

I thought when I started this book that this would be the easiest area to write. As I have gone through the different stages of solving issues, I now find myself having difficulty in what to put as examples.

So here we go:

These are just a few cases that may relate to the average family or individual that might resemble some to the difficulties you might be having. I will give the background then the solution. These are basic problems without going into full detail in every case.

Background

A client came to me in a very stressful state. He had been married for 12 years, thought his marriage was fine until he came home one day to find a note saying she had found someone else and had left him. As both were working and bringing a joint income into the household, as well as having a house in joint names, he realised all the loans and credit cards were in his name. As his ex partner was not contributing to the Mortgage and with only having £100 left for food and running a car to get to work after all expenses of the house were taken into account, he had to decide what to do.

Solution

After looking at his £47,000 level of unsecured debt, an IVA was out of the question due to a low surplus income, a DMP was looked at and unfortunately once again, due to funds, this was unacceptable as he would be paying for ever. He also decided, after getting a redemption statement from the Mortgage Company, that the value of the house would not cover the outstanding balance, so he wanted to give the property back to the lender. It was agreed that he would look for a smaller property and privately rent. The outcome was he went Bankrupt, handed the keys back and added the possible short fall for any negative equity. He is now legally debt free.

Background

A client had a business with a shop on a High Street and due to the recession, fell behind with rent as well as the lease and was continuously overdrawn with the bank. As she tried to support her business, hoping trade would improve, she started to use her personal credit cards to live and pay creditors. Once we got involved, we looked at her liabilities and found she had signed a long lease paying over £2,000 per month. We tried to negotiate with the landlord to reduce the monthly agreement; unfortunately they were unhelpful and started legal proceedings.

Solution

As her debts including the remaining lease of over £97,000 and she was renting a private house, we suggested Bankruptcy and this option was taken. Just to expand on this client, she was allowed to be Self Employed after Bankruptcy and found a smaller shop to trade from and is clear to start again.

Background

Another client worked abroad earning fantastic money (over £100,000 per year). He was sending money to his wife and he thought he had no debts whatsoever back home including no Mortgage. When he was made redundant two years ago, near to Christmas, he thought he would buy his wife a nice present and went to the bank. He tried to withdraw money and found there was an overdraft. When he asked to see the manager, he found he also had a Mortgage as well as credit cards he had no knowledge of. He found his wife had been living it up while he was out of the country and had forged his signature for the cards as well as the Mortgage. The client started divorce proceedings but didn't know what to do about the debts. Eventually the house was given back to the Mortgage Company and during this period his wife went Bankrupt leaving the joint Mortgage his responsibility.

Solution

We first of all advised the client to get the Police involved to prove he couldn't have signed for the Mortgage when he worked away for 6 months of the year. Due to having children, he didn't want to pursue this action for their sake. We looked at his job prospects and as there was a possibility, due to the down turn in the labour market for his specialist trade, his income would be drastically reduced for the next few years, the options offered were a DMP and bankruptcy. He took the latter as a DMP was going to take far too long to pay off.

Background

This couple came to me with debts of over £40,000. They had a house with a Mortgage of £200,000 which they were trying to sell valued at £300,000 but it needed a lot of repairs. Their debts were caused by having to fly their son back from Australia due to a serious accident, as well as paying for a life threatening operation. Just after this event the husband lost his well paid job and the debts mounted; they had, for the previous two years, negotiated with their Creditors. Unfortunately the Creditors were adamant they wanted an increase in the monthly contributions. With only one income into the household this was impossible.

Solution

We used a third party to set up a DMP to take the pressure of the clients and asked them to change their telephone numbers as the Creditors were constantly ringing. We also in addition to the DMP, put a claim in for their credit cards and loans to see if any agreements had any flaws in them. When the agreements came back from the lenders, the claims company informed the couple they had been paying PPI on three agreements that they didn't know about. This resulted in compensation of £15,000 which went towards offering the major Creditors full and final settlements to reduce the outstanding debt. Their debts are now easily managed via a DMP paying £250 per month; the house is safe and they are happy with our actions. May I point out, if they had gone to the CAB or a number of other companies, they wouldn't have been offered the variety of options and solutions we came up with.

Background

This situation gives me a lot of satisfaction in fighting for a cause when the lender would not listen.

A client was made Bankrupt due to owing the Inland Revenue money; he was jointly named on a Mortgaged property. (Please note this couple were in their 60s). As the Official Receivers demanded part of the equity from the house to pay into this estate, his wife had to sign what was called a Self Certified Mortgage to release equity. Due to this action this would allow him to stay Self Employed to earn an income to pay the Mortgage. Everything was going well paying the Mortgage on time until, a year later; his wife was rushed to hospital with a life threatening illness. Due to this, his thoughts understandably were for his wife's health and he was at her bedside constantly for over 3 months. During this time he didn't earn any money and fell behind with the Mortgage. As we have said previously, subprime lenders used to start repossession after two months and this was the case in this instance.

Solution

I first of all tried to contact the lender to stop the repossession action, but they wouldn't talk to me as we could not get a signed authority as she was in a coma. Due to this we had to go to a Court hearing and took evidence of a signed doctor's report. The lender tried to object to my presence; fortunately my reputation with some of the Judges went in my favour and we not only stopped the action by getting the warrant suspended, but due to the lenders arrogant actions the Judge would not allow the costs involved to be added to the balance. We have since had to go back to Court on a number of occasions as his wife has had many recurring problems. Fortunately the lender now talks to me if there is a problem with payment and doesn't take any further action as I resolve the situation.

Background

A young man wanted help with his debts as he had been gambling and lived with his well to do parents who were very concerned that he owed over £40,000 to his bank and various credit cards. Although he had stopped gambling and was attending gamblers anonymous, he was on a very low income and borrowed money from other family members.

Solution

We looked at many solutions for this client and talked in depth with his parents. We suggested Bankruptcy, a DMP for a £200pm (that's all he could afford) and a one off IVA funded by his family. The family wanted to pay the Creditors a decent dividend but also stop their son being able to borrow further money, to teach him a lesson. The DMP was going to be a very long commitment; Bankruptcy was going to put the home address in the paper which the parents didn't want and so it was agreed a one off IVA be put forward to the Creditors where the parents would take out a loan for £15,000 and the Creditors accepted. (There was an agreement drawn up whereby the son would pay the parents £200 per month towards the loan taken out).

Background

A Director of a company had used his credit cards and his personal overdraft to fund a large contract. After the job was completed, his client went into receivership leaving the company with large debts as well as personal financial problems. The client required immediate funds to pay off the company overdraft and so, in desperation, contacted a lender advertising in a national newspaper which promised £30,000 within three weeks (the interest on this secured loan was 26 %!). Although at the time he accepted in desperation and agreed he could pay the monthly commitment, he wasn't told PPI had been included in the loan adding a further £10,000. 2 years later when he asked for help with his finances, we found he and his wife had over £60,000 of debt on credit cards and loans etc, as well as a personal overdraft for £15,000 which the bank was demanding or was going to court to get security.

Solution

We looked at all the various options available as this was a complex case. When we discovered the level of debt as well as the outstanding balance on the Mortgage and Secured loan, we suggested the following: a five year IVA with a fourth year valuation to remortgage the property up to 85% of the value of the house, or remortgaging the property to consolidate the secured loans as well taking a further £26,000 to offer a one off IVA to Creditors. It was agreed to take the latter. The Mortgage offer was put in place and the Insolvency Company set up a Creditors meeting showing the offer which was accepted. Many might not agree with this action, but the client saved over £200 per month on secured loan repayments by consolidating the interest rate to 7% at the time and you have to remember there was a threat by the bank to put a charge on the house, so we think this was a more favourable solution. Our client was legally debt free showing an IVA had been successfully completed on his credit file. The client also claimed on the PPI and received a refund.

Background

A couple had debts between them, the majority in her name (£30,000), spent mostly on clothes as well as holidays and high living and Mr, having £4,000, who seemed to be very cautious as to what he could afford. As they had a house worth £105,000 with a 95% Mortgage, we had to look at different areas to resolve the situation, bearing in mind they had reasonably paid jobs.

Solution

Once again we looked at the future prospects of the couple making sure their jobs were quite safe. We offered a variety of options: a 5yr IVA paying £225pm for Mrs and a £100pm DMP for Mr. We also suggested Mrs could go Bankrupt and Mr would have to find from family approximately £2,000 to buy out his wife's equity whilst still having to pay into a DMP, and the final alternative was she did an IVA and Mr paid his Creditors as usual. The latter was chosen by the client.

Background

We came across a couple who had remortgaged their house with a certain lender who offered 125% Mortgages. (House valued at the time at £200,000), and the balance outstanding was £250,000. On top of this, the clients had debts to the tune of £40,000 as well as a further secured loan of £20,000 due to a failed business. So the couple had negative equity of £70,000 and an additional £40,000 unsecured.

Solutions

As we have said previously, this is a difficult decision as to whether to keep the property or not. The client was advised to go Bankrupt and to find rented accommodation, as staying would have meant years of struggling with the high payments on the Mortgage. This they accepted and put in to their Bankruptcy the negative equity owed to the lender leaving them debt free.

Background

A single person came to us after graduating and getting a reasonable job; she had a very large student loan as well as many credit cards and loans she had taken out for her boyfriend as his credit wasn't particularly good (and of course he loved her, didn't he?) You know what's coming next. Yes he left her taking the goods she had bought him, as well as the car that she found out was in his name.

Solution

Due to her having a reasonable surplus income, it was agreed that an IVA over 5 years was her best and only option to stop Creditors harassing her, as well as freezing the interest. (and learned a lesson in love) Of course the student loan still had to be paid as this is not allowed in a IVA.

Testimonials

The following are just a few of the many clients who have sent messages of thanks; they are their own words, not mine:

How can I thank you for all your hard work and advice. I was made Bankrupt in February 2007, I, saw a Judge at Court and showed them your papers following which a paper was stamped all in one afternoon. I am so grateful to you.
ML

We don't know how we would have got through all this without you pulling everything together for us. Thanks to you for all your patience and good advice and all the support you have given us. If I win the lottery I will throw a big party and you will be the guest of honor – you deserve it. Keep up the good work.
O&A

Thank you for doing everything for us. We will never be able to thank you enough. They say everyone has a Guardian Angel – you were definitely ours.
MH

You have really helped me to plan and given us a far greater level of optimism for our potential relocation to Australia. All the best to you
BS

Thank you to you and everyone in your Company that helped me through my worst experience of my life including paperwork and your kind advice on the telephone which I appreciate so much.

Chris took away all the anxiety and worry which going Bankrupt caused me and has basically given me my life back. All his staff were always Courteous and helpful. I personally cannot recommend Chris and his Company highly enough.
GK

Thank you so much for giving us the most positive advice and putting our minds at ease. Chris was always very pleasant and myself and my wife will pass Chris and his Company onto all our family and friends.
KC

Following a number of bad experiences with other organisations I came across Chris's number. Since then I have received nothing but good advice and hopefully all will be resolved at my Creditors Meeting. Once again I send many thanks.
GK

I would like to take the opportunity to thank you very much for your help and advice given to us. We would like to wish you and your Team continued success in helping people like us. Thank you from the bottom of our hearts.
Mr & Mrs A

Following your advice I find I now have peace of mind at last and I realise it was the only way out for me. Chris, I won't ever forget you.

RA

We would like to thank you for your kindness and all the help you have given us. We feel much better now and appreciate everything you have done for us.

Mr & Mrs S

Have you ever been caught up in a dispute where there seems to be no way out? How many times have you sat in a solicitor's office knowing that each minute costs you money? Has your family suffered hardship because of dishonest practices by others?

LISTEN UP:

I am a company Director who reached retirement age. The co Director in the company promised the earth and delivered nothing. He made it very clear that he was solely taking on the tasks of running the company his way.

More than two years later, with a number of abortive negotiation attempts colluding with the beneficiaries, being the solicitor as well as the accountant, I had nowhere to go.

After all this time my dilemma was:

I had no pension, my investment in the company being a Director's loan was being whittled away and there was a threat against the return of the balance outstanding. Believe me I was desperate.

In a two hour conversation with the author of this book, he bought elements from his lifetime of experience gave me concise instructions on how to deal with a less than cooperative individual who had assumed a megalomaniac attitude to rip off a former loyal business partner.

What a transformation! From being suppressed, I now have the upper hand with all the aces for negotiating and believe you me I will use them to address all the problems and heartaches created by a person I once considered to be a friend!

Chris is a gentleman who spends most of his time generally looking after and advised people who are caught up in the debt minefield, whether as an individual or solving problems in business.

I wish I had known him two years before I did, I would have saved thousands on fees that I have paid to solicitors, who in the end gave up not knowing what else they could do after sending standard letters, keeping to their own remit of going so far without any new energising ways to think outside the normal way of claiming or a new action for what I was owed.

My wife has said why didn't we meet him ages ago, and for the first time since this traumatic experience started we are both chuckling to ourselves about the future events that will unfold in our favour.

If you have a business problem in trying to get money owed or have problems financially within a business or company, contact Chris in confidence as I'm sure he will be able to guide you to a satisfactory conclusion.
KF

Many thanks for all your help and understanding during the past few weeks. Best Wishes
LN

I would like to thank you and your Team for everything you have done and your support through this for me and my family. At first we didn't know what to do but with your support we can now start afresh.

DT

I wish to thank you for all your help and support. I know I couldn't have got through this time without your help. It was like living a nightmare but you gave me the confidence to get through it. Your staff were also so caring and helpful and I will never forget all of you. May God bless you all and success in everything you do.

TS

Thank you very much for all your help and support, for being there for us 100% of the way and allaying all my fears. You were so truthful and honest from the start. You went above and beyond your duty to help us and you are a genuinely nice guy who cares for his clients. You are a credit to your Company and we will not hesitate to recommend you to anyone experiencing financial problems. Thanks for everything Chris.

Mr & Mrs F

I am writing to thank you for giving me a better life. When I first rang your number I had no idea how much it would change my life. I was terrified when I went to Court but both you and Steve were by my side at Court to support me. The relief was amazing when it was all over. Because of your help I don't need to worry about bills and I am now able to save a little and treat my grandchildren. Thank you for everything.

HW

Dear Chris. Thank you very much for your help and support during my Bankruptcy, your advice proved to be invaluable and I would have no hesitation in recommending your services.

PG

May I first of all thank your team with helping to settle my nerves through a very complicated financial situation; I have to say although I was worried about paying a fee for your services I found it amazing that you answered the phone over the weekend as well as late into many a night. It was well worth it and I know I was a pain, but you made me feel a special person. What amazed me even more was helping to put a background story of the events leading up to my predicament and because you listened, you built up a picture of what had happened to such an extent I had a tear in my eye reading about myself. I know you are writing a book and I give my permission if you wish to use this letter as a testimonial. You are one of the most caring people I have ever talked to.

TS

After a messy split with my ex partner I was left in dire financial circumstances. To make matters worse I had recently became unemployed during the recession. I had credit card, personal loans and a Mortgage which I could no longer afford to pay. It took a while before I realised there were people who could help and I was advised to contact a debt help organisation. I contacted the Citizens Advice who gave me the number of a few agencies. After initial contact with them I waited and waited for a reply. 3 weeks and nothing was happening. In the meantime my debtors were getting more and more aggressive with threatening letters and constant harassment with phone calls.

It was sheer luck that I came by Chris's company. A friend of a friend recommended and I gave them a ring. Chris came to my house that very night! He helped me set out an income budget, then got me started with a debt management plan. Not only did he help me set things up but he was also available for advice when I needed it!

Now almost a year later he has helped me once again with a particular aggressive debtor who was taking me to Court applying for a CCJ despite regular payments being made on time. He fought on behalf of me in Court and stopped the CCJ as well as the costs the lender wanted to add. I can honestly say that if I hadn't met Chris my situation would have been unbearable and I owe him a ton of thanks for his patience, knowledge and friendly advice.

MP

The above testimonials and my passion to help people are what keeps me in this business. I can't operate as an automaton. Each case is individual and anyone who struggles with such delicate money problems, deserves to be treated with compassion and respect. With my vast and varied experience I believe I am one of the best Debt Counsellors you are likely to find. My ability to problem solve a financial situation offering as many options as possible for the client to understand and decide leads me on to my next quest of helping a wider audience.

The Future

There will be a minimum of approximately 3 further books that will be published within the next year or so. These will be on more specific areas as follows:

Due to the number of expats in Europe, as well as around the world who are now struggling with financial issues in today's economic climate, a book will be published as to what we can do to resolving these types of problems, hopefully and in many cases without you having to come back to the UK.

As I have run a number of businesses, I feel that I have a vast knowledge that I can pass on to others in plain language for those who are registered now, or might be thinking of setting up soon, as well as the company Director of a private registered limited company and the good things and the pitfalls you have to be aware of. It will go into being a Bank guarantor, Accountants, if you should or should not be a limited company as well as looking at the other side of the fence in getting paid by your Creditors and what you can do to safeguard yourself financially.

As the market changes, a sequel to this book will be published as well as other changes that might happen during the economic times that this as well as other countries will have to overcome.

Hopefully by the time this book is published there will be other avenues for helping the many in need of advice.

There will be a website that will be on a membership basis where individuals will pay a membership to go on line and ask live questions for me and my staff to answer. The advantage is others who are on line will hear the reply, widening their own knowledge.

It is proposed that the following fee will be for a one month membership so you can come on line on the dates and times advertised (minimum 2 times a week) as many times as you like to ask questions and listen to the answer.

Yes there is a charge, but when you think, other organisations don't have the far reaching knowledge I have to offer. I think it is a very fair price to pay knowing there will be someone to help you.

If you sought advice from a solicitor, they could charge up to £150/200 per hour and you would have to wait for an appointment,

You could go to a free organisation like the CAB who will book you in for a fantastic 20 minute meeting (How many questions would you be able to ask in this period of time?) during the day of course to help you (being sarcastic). "O" and you might have to wait up to 3 weeks for the appointment, and also bear in mind, you might have to have a day off work or both of you if you're a couple in this dilemma. If this is the case, to give you an example: if you are both full time on a minimum wage of say £6 per hour you will lose £48 each, at a time when you need every penny that counts when you're struggling with finances.

If you went into a DMP paying £100pm you will be charged £35pm and the first two months in total £550 for the first year and you won't know if it was the right decision. You might do a IVA over 5yrs in total over the term paying approximately £7,000. Again, was the best product for you?

So in my opinion, I feel the advice charges set out below are extremely reasonable for the knowledge I have in solving problems. May I add further that if you wanted our services or help completing certain paperwork for a particular product, we will deduct what you have paid to join the forum from our standard fee.

The Fees

Re Monthly Video Conferencing Membership

As I try to help all walks of life, there are categories depending on your income and proof of your financial situation will be required. The fee will be based on the household gross income/circumstances. You will need to follow the link on my website or log on to www.debtadvicebychrisjary.co.uk and follow the instructions.

For the unfortunate who are both unemployed	£30
Couples working that have a joint income that's less than £25,000 PA,	£50
Couples/Individuals with earnings of up to £50,000	£70
Couples/Individuals earning over £50,000	£90
Self Employed Individuals	£100

Self Employed with partner working with joint
income of £50,000   £100

Company Directors who no doubt will have more
complicated issues will pay   £120

DVD

There will also be a DVD for people to watch if they are not
into reading which will give the basic of what we have said
in this book. Log on to www.debtadvicebychrisjary.co.uk

Ebook

Again this will be available as an eBook within the first
part of 2011 for anyone who might want to read this via
the technology we have of today around the world please
log on to www.debtadvicebychrisjary.co.uk.

Conclusion

I hope you will take on board a lot about what I have said in this book, hopefully giving you a better understanding of the different areas of help and awareness as to what to look out for.

However, if you need further advice our details are as follows and we have designated numbers for some of the common products:

How to Contact Us

Address: Action for Debt
Chris Jary
Office 3,
108B Newgate Street
Bishop Auckland
Co. Durham
DL14 7EQ

Telephone No: Main office number   01388 608955
0330 330 3209
0845 6437820

Web Address: www.actionfordebt.com

Product/Purchase Website
www.debtadvicebychrisjary.co.uk

Email address: advice@actionfordebt.com

Product telephone numbers:

IVA	0330 330 3203
Debt Management Plans	0330 330 3204
Bankruptcy	0330 330 3205
House Repossession	0330 330 3206
Full & Final Settlements	0330 330 3207